CONTENTS

Understanding Codependency

The Science Behind It and How to Break the Cycle

Sharon Wegscheider-Cruse
& Joseph Cruse, M.D.

Health Communications, Inc.
Deerfield Beach, Florida

www.hcibooks.com

Dedicated to the pioneers in the
field of addictive disease who recognized
that more than one person is affected
by any singular addiction.
They represent, "Those who make paths,
not just follow them . . ."

Library of Congress Cataloging-in-Publication Data

Cruse, Joseph R., 1930-
    Understanding codependency : the science behind it and how to break the cycle /
Joseph Cruse, Sharon Wegscheider-Cruse. Updated and expanded ed.
        p. cm.
    Includes bibliographical references.
    ISBN-13: 978-0-7573-1617-3 (trade paper)
    ISBN-10: 0-7573-1617-4 (trade paper)
    ISBN-13: 978-0-7573-1618-0 (e-book)
    ISBN-10: 0-7573-1618-2 (e-book)
    1. Codependency.   I. Wegscheider-Cruse, Sharon, 1938-   II. Title.
RC569.5C63W34   2012
616.86'19—dc23   2012010530

Publisher: Health Communications, Inc.
            3201 S.W. 15th Street
            Deerfield Beach, FL 33442–8190

Interior design and formatting by Lawna Patterson Oldfield

INTRODUCTION TO THE SECOND EDITION

Codependency: Defining the Word

Thirty-one years ago alcohol rehab facilities began to promote their treatment facilities and extend their treatment techniques to individuals who were dependent on (addicted to) substances other than alcohol (heroin, cocaine, narcotic/sedative medications, etc.). In an effort to describe these individuals, the terms *chemically dependent* and *chemical dependency* became popular.

People were confused and upset by the use of the term *chemical dependency*. "Of course, I am dependent on chemicals, just as I am to the soap in my dishwasher, the rubber in my tires, and the air that I breathe. What a silly term—no clinical help at all!" But the term has stuck and is in popular usage by both professionals and the public at large.

Codependency

Prior to the use of the term *chemical dependency*, family members, particularly spouses, were described as *co-alcoholics*. Therefore, when the term *chemically dependent* began to be used, it became almost second nature to describe the spouse and family members as *codependents*.

The word "codependency" has been shortened (codep, co-), restricted (only for the co-alcoholic or co-addict), and expanded into general usage to describe almost any persistent preoccupation a person may have. It has been changed from a hyphenated word, "co-dependency," which indicates a co-occurring event, to a nonhyphenated, single word, "codependency," which indicates a stand-alone event. No wonder there is confusion, especially since the meaning of the original word never actually received complete agreement from the professional treatment field or individuals in the "recovery" arena.

The stand-alone word "codependency" is probably the form of the word that is most popular. It can still be used to describe a co-alcoholic or a codependent, and it can also be used to describe individuals with dependencies and addictions that evolve from negative or excessive involvement in other areas. Examples of this include behaviors or activities that capture a person's interest and detract from their usual environments of family, friends, and work, such as gambling (in person and online), technology, sexual acting out (affairs, online pornography, etc.), overeating or not eating, and so on, to name just a few. Dependence on or addiction to these activities results in an emotional divorce from family, friends, and coworkers, and the individual figuratively moves in with a mistress who is represented by the behavior or activity. This is recognized as an actual addiction when it reaches advanced stages. It is called *process addiction* (or *behavioral addiction*).

Process addiction is a recurring, compulsive condition whereby a person engages in an unrestrained, specific activity despite harmful consequences to his or her health, mental state, or community life. Behavioral addiction, like codependency, is considered harmful if it results in negative consequences for the person and for those with whom they associate. People can be addicted to gambling, food, sex, pornography, computers and the Internet, video games, work, exercise, spiritual obsession (as opposed to religious devotion), shopping, cutting, and pain.

Using the term *codependency* has certain benefits. It can act as a shortcut to understanding the nature of addiction. But giving a name to the state of being codependent does not necessarily mean that there is an immediate or even effective permanent solution for it, so the term must be used with caution. There are a large number of therapies available for many different mental health conditions, including codependency. Some are helpful and some are not.

In summary, codependency is still frequently the "diagnosis" attached to the behavior, thoughts, or "condition" of a person who is involved in a highly dependent relationship with someone who requires extra care or vigilance, such as a practicing alcoholic or drug addict. Even so, it has been difficult for the treatment field to convince the decision-makers that here, indeed, is a treatable condition that can be diagnosed, has evidence-based treatment available, and for which therapists should receive reimbursement.

The *New Oxford American Dictionary* defines codependency as "excessive emotional or psychological reliance on a partner, typically a partner who requires support due to an illness or addiction," and codependent as "1 (dependent on/ upon) contingent on or determined by; 2 a person who relies on another, esp. a family member, for financial, emotional, or other support; unable to do without: *people dependent on drugs*" (authors' emphasis).

Now, with the passage of time and our recent experiences and new discoveries regarding brain function in compulsive and addictive diseases, our understanding of codependency has improved. It is possible to relate the dynamics of codependency to existing knowledge regarding brain function, personality characteristics, childhood trauma, and social influences. Acceptance and recognition of codependency has increased.

Behavior that appears briefly and with little impact on the life of an individual might be termed "transient" or "temporary." The distinction is mentioned here because "That's codependent!" is frequently used in casual conversations, where it might not apply to the more recent definition of the condition.

Codependency Minor

Behavior that is of concern to the individual per se and not necessarily to those around him or her might be termed "minor." Individuals with codependency minor are usually experiencing unease rather than disease. They know that something is amiss or going amiss and they have some insight into it. They have enough self-worth that seeking help and guidance is the first thing they do. They might be termed "the worried well." They profit greatly from their realistic self-intervention.

Codependency Major

Codependent behavior that is seriously impacting the life of an individual and those in the individual's environment (home, work, social circle, etc.) might be termed as "major."

These individuals have developed enough of a denial system that complications are occurring in numerous areas of their lives. They deny the severity or even the existence of their problems. They externalize their beliefs as to the cause of their problems. They develop compulsions that help to suppress the negative feelings they have. They believe the solutions reside outside themselves, and they live in an "if only" world. "Everything would be okay, if only . . ." They might be described quite accurately as "the walking wounded."

This is not meant to label those with mental illness or those who require counseling and guidance, as we all do from time to time, but rather this is an effort to place a condition in its rightful place in a continuum of health and illness in their varying degrees. If we can be clear in our use of the word, then we can communicate with more accuracy, without judgment or labels, and individuals who read this will be empowered to do what is necessary to improve their lives and find solutions to their problems.

We know there is a group of individuals who may have serious and fixed thoughts and behaviors that led them into complications at an early age. *These are now expanded to include children from any home where any addiction is present or where even nonaddicted but dysfunctional behavior from other sources occurs.* Early onset often results in major codependency. Some children grow up with resiliency and enter adulthood with a strong sense of self. A small percentage are fortunate enough to have been through formal therapy or training for codependency, and they too can become very resilient.

Other children who live in the midst of dysfunctional families often grow up with major living problems and usually do not begin their search for help until they are adults. There are treatment and support organizations for them, such as the National Association of Children of Alcoholics (NACoA, in Washington, D.C.) and several 12-step support groups, including Adult Children of Alcoholics (ACoA), Codependents Anonymous (CoDA), and Alateen/Alanon.

All of us have mental, emotional, and behavioral problems that occur throughout our lives and that require attention and resolution from time to time. These problems are a natural part of life, and each of us is responsible for seeking the solutions to the problems that arise in our lives. We need knowledge, sometimes outside help, and certainly a belief that while there may be problems, they can be fixed.

Welcome to the Revised Edition of
Understanding Codependency

This edition contains new material that expands on and validates the information given in the first edition, as well as some editorial revisions to the text. A new chapter on codependency and the functions of the brain has been added, and we have also added text that confirms that symptoms of codependency are Brain Events and what we call complications of codependency are Life Events. Additionally, another new chapter, "Sorting Out Codependency," gives readers more in-depth information that will help them discern if codependency is impacting their lives and what to do about it in terms of treatment and recovery. Last, a section containing the references for the new edition and an updated list of resources are presented.

CHAPTER 1

Codependency and the Brain

Until the 1970s, most of the research interest in addictive diseases, especially alcoholism, centered on the liver. Investigators felt that if the reasons for the serious impact that alcohol had on the liver were known, the basis for alcoholism would become clear. University researchers and government agencies received grants to carry out investigations that centered on the liver. Psychologists, psychiatrists, and other therapists were caught up in psychodynamics, behavioral therapy, psychoanalysis, and other theories of the mind in an effort to help those addicted to alcohol and other drugs.

Brain Functions

Meanwhile, brain researchers discovered previously unknown chemicals, functions, and anatomical relationships in the brain that affected the thoughts, behaviors, and feelings of individuals—the same "mind-related" entities that the psychiatric, psychological, and therapeutic disciplines had been struggling to understand for centuries. A collision course between the various disciplines became inevitable. Brain chemistry, real-time scanning, and other imagery revealed some of the close relationships between the brain and addictive, compulsive behavior. A fusion bomb of research exploded, and the fields of psychiatry, psychology, and behavioral medicine zeroed in on the brain. Dr. Mark Gold, professor of psychiatry at the University of Florida, College of Medicine, happily announced, "The field of psychiatry finally has an organ to work with!"

Organs have one or more functions in the body. The pancreas is an example of an organ that performs at least two major functions: it manufactures digestive juices and it manufactures and releases insulin and other chemicals that our bodies need to work efficiently. If we looked at the brain metaphorically in terms of its functions, we could describe it as the thinker or the mind, the doer, the behaver, the feeler, and the pleasure seeker, among others. These functions are more difficult to measure than most other organ functions. For example, it is easy to measure urine output and composition as an indicator of kidney function. It is more difficult to exactly measure a thought or the emotions of joy or anger.

Pleasure/Relief Center

We are still learning the various "outputs" and composition of the brain and how they affect what the body does. There is a "pleasure center" (which could also be referred to as a relief center) in the brain that is primarily involved in setting up pathways that result in addiction and addictive behaviors. This center receives and sends its messages (commands) up, around, down, and all over the body thousands of times per second on thousands of pathways. If we could light it up, its activity would dwarf the busiest streaming decorative digital billboards in Times Square or on the Las Vegas Strip.

The brain has a multitude of different centers for many different functions. Rather than describe all of these centers, their locations (anatomy), and the chemicals (neurotransmitters, hormones) and nerves that serve them, it is simpler to just use the concept of pathways that the brain uses to communicate with itself and the rest of the body. These pathways are used over and over again for a variety of functions. New pathways are constantly created; old pathways stay lit as long as they are used; inactive brain pathways can be dimmed, but probably never completely disappear, because some old pathways can be easily reignited.

Creating, dimming, and reigniting pathways occur constantly in the brain thousands of times a second. The brain is thinking up, forgetting, and remembering at breakneck speeds all day long: one hundred billion nerve cells, one hundred trillion connections, and hundreds of "feel-good" chemicals that are released into the body indicate that our marvelous brains can do all of this.

The pathways that are formed in our brains throughout life as we live and learn in the midst of our experiences influence how we respond to the world around us. But our brains can mislead us. Why do our brains tell us we "have to have" a certain outcome, a certain relationship, a certain food or amount of food, and/or a certain sense of power and reputation, when many times we don't? Every time we find relief or pleasure, a pleasure pathway is brightened up. Even when it is at our own expense in some way, our pleasure centers are stimulated and our brains now say, "Do it again and again and again. Don't stop, or I will make you so uncomfortable that you will feel withdrawal, anxiety, sadness, loneliness, and pain."

Every time we are rewarded for something we have done or have sacrificed some aspect of our lives for another person's benefit (whether they needed it or not), our brains send out the same message: "This is great! Get me more, more, more! Don't stop, or I will send you into letdown/withdrawal!" (For a graphic example of this, see Figure 2.1 in Chapter 2, "The Codependency Trap," on page 32.)

The more people focus outside of themselves for their self-worth, and the longer their codependent life continues, the brighter the codependent pleasure/relief pathways become. These pathways can be dimmed and lose their power when a person begins recovery. To remain "turned on," pathways require steady exposure (the timing and amounts of exposure required vary among individuals). To remain "turned down," addictive pleasure pathways require abstinence. When codependent people abstain from whatever behavior they have been using to avoid pain (alcohol, drugs, food, etc.), they have the ability to recover, as long as they continue to remain abstinent.

It is helpful to understand how these pathways in the brain work as you undertake your own recovery:

- New pathways (recovery pathways) are created by constructive new thoughts, events, behaviors, and emotions.

- Dimmed pathways (recovery) can occur by not reinforcing an already existing pathway.

- Reignited pathways (relapse) can recur from old codependent thoughts, events, behaviors, and emotions.

Suggested Progressive Mental Disorders

Codependency can be a precursor to other distinctive, perhaps addictive, disorders. It can evolve into full-blown, discreet, diagnosable mental health issues. Codependency increases in its intensity, and it begins to purify itself into more serious, specific sets of repetitive behaviors and symptoms. Some of these become recognizable personality disorders or other mental health disorders.

We are all born with personalities, and they are each as unique as our fingerprints. While there are many wonderful components of personality, mental disorders can evolve from some personality traits. Traits can protect us and be useful to us when they are not used excessively. Three traits that are sometimes useful to us but are frequently used to excess by codependents are our *avoidant, dependent,* and *obsessive-compulsive* traits.

In codependency, these personality traits become seriously exaggerated and lead to anxious or fearful traits. Anxious or fearful personality traits can lead to emotional, dramatic, or erratic personality traits and then to actual personality disorders. Severe eccentric or odd personality disorders may progress to overt mental disorders. It can be argued that any of these conditions appear to arise de novo without any preceding disorder. Why do we keep increasing codependent thoughts and behaviors? Because codependency, addictions, and addictive behaviors result in *tolerance*.

Tolerance

Tolerance occurs in the brain and results in diminished relief from the same behavior we have been repeating again and again. (See Figure 1.1 on page 17.) We "get used to it." Therefore, our codependent behavior has to increase for relief to be regained. The most common increases include frequency, duration, intensity, and variation of the behavior.

- If we start getting less relief from our negative emotions by volunteering once a week, we need to increase it to more days.

- If we start getting less relief from visiting our children, we need to increase our length of stay with them.

- If we start getting less relief from a holiday, we need to pack more into it.
- If we start getting less relief from one hobby, we need to take up two or three additional ones.

With the increases due to tolerance, the progression of codependency accelerates.

Withdrawal Symptoms

Withdrawal symptoms occur when the comforting effects of an activity or a chemical stop having an influence on us. Withdrawal symptoms can be quite bothersome, both to you and to those close to you. Symptoms of anxiety, craving, nervousness, preoccupation, loss of concentration, and irritation arise. The feel-good chemicals we stimulated are no longer around and we crave them. Of course, we can have these emotional reactions and pain reactions at other times. These reactions are for general use, not just in withdrawal. The more attention given to them, the more they bother us.

Since stopping self-sacrificing behavior is one of the steps of recovery from codependency, withdrawal must be managed as comfortably and safely as possible. This is true for codependents, alcoholics, and drug addicts. *Fact*: Withdrawal is a struggle between you and your brain, not you and another person, situation, or event. Your brain nags enough to finally cause you to shout, "Shut up! Stop nagging me!"

And sometimes, sadly, you say, "Okay, okay, I give in; here is your next fix!"

Relapse

If you have been able to begin the road to recovering from codependency, but you return to your old behaviors again, the pathway of relapse brightens up. Relapsing back into codependency is easy—with just a little "slip," everything starts over. This indicates that the original pathways were just dimmed rather than eliminated. Dimmed pathways are just "lying in wait" and will reignite if exposed again.

Remember, the relief one feels from a relapse or a "slip" is not due to just a return of a temporary "good" feeling. Your codependent behavior is acting like a medication for relief of the withdrawal symptoms your brain is causing. It is almost as though our brains are acting like spoiled little kids; many an alcoholic and addict have been called just that.

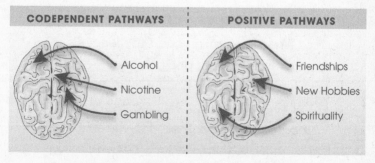

Figure 1.1. Pathways Ignited in the Brain

Also, remember that new experiences and new information constantly create new pathways in our marvelous brains. As we free ourselves from codependency pathways, we need new, strong, positive pathways to replace them. A slogan or mantra (a Hindu or Buddhist saying or prayer that is repeated over and over as an aid in concentration or focus) that we can repeatedly say to our brains is "Hey, I don't do this anymore! Get it!" Each time this is said, a recovery pathway grows brighter and brighter until it becomes a powerful part of us. Soon our brains start "getting clean." We move from the shadow of codependency into a more comfortable life of self-worth and self-determination.

Now that we have explored the function of the brain and how pathways are formed, in Chapter 2 we will look more closely at the interaction between our own manufactured brain chemicals and how repetitive behavior stimulates the brain to establish compulsive and addictive behavior processes.

> When information and experiences are repeated over and over again, and when they are impactful, interesting, or important to us, we create strong, positive pathways. These then influence how we think, feel, and behave.

CHAPTER 2

The Codependency Trap

So often we hear codependents say:

1. Why do I keep doing the same things over and over?

2. Why can't I stop thinking about certain things?

3. If I look so good, why do I feel so bad?

4. Why can't I stop hurting myself with drugs,
   cigarettes, people, food, alcohol, gambling, and (fill
   in the blank)?

These answers are best found in understanding the brain.
When we understand how our brains function, we can begin
to understand and treat codependency.

To completely understand the dynamics of codependency,
we need to understand a new science. This science has many
different names, such as neuropsychology, psychoneu-
robiology, and/or neurochemistry. In his book *Molecules
of the Mind*, Jon Franklin, Pulitzer Prize–winning author,
describes brain function by saying that "The basis of this
new discipline is the perception that human thought, emotion, and behavior results from the inner play of molecules
across the surface of brain cells."

The brain provides a model of function and disease—a
paradigm. Thomas Kuhn gives importance to the term *paradigm* in his book *The Structure of Scientific Revolutions* when
he says, "Without commitment to a paradigm [model], there
can be no science."

We have found it necessary when designing a treatment program for codependency that a scientific model be
established for the purpose of providing us, our patients, our
staff, and our colleagues with the necessary degree of speci-
ficity, accountability, and predictability.

Is Codependency a Brain Disorder?

Immediately the reader may feel some discomfort with the concept of mental illness or codependency defined basically as a brain disorder. Those of you who were trained in the 1950s to the 1970s are familiar with the conflict that exists between the scientific community and the adaptive or humanistic community. The division between these disciplines is likened to the differences in the disciplines between Eastern and Western medicine.

Those in the West direct their efforts toward precise cause and effect, signs and symptoms, and continual self-evaluation. There tends to be an appreciation of the chronology of events, staging, and classifications. In the East, the new brain information supports much of what practitioners there have known for centuries through the practice of healing, meditation, and prayer. In this country we have seen the mainstream of scientific concern and 12-step programs merge closer. It seems as though the Nature versus Nurture controversy is becoming more Nature plus Nurture.

Dr. Joseph T. Quail of Johns Hopkins School of Medicine states, "With advances in research on the brain over the last 15 years, we have now reached the point that neuroscience can justifiably be considered the biomedical foundation of psychiatry." In no other area is this information as easily understood as it is in learning to understand codependency.

In codependency, it is the interaction between one's own manufactured "brain chemicals" (having to do with our reinforcement center) and one's behavior that stimulates the brain to establish compulsive and addictive behavior processes. Many have thought that codependency has been due to life's problems, such as living with an alcoholic or addict, having low self-worth, being from an alcoholic family, and so on, but it's the other way around. Because we have a brain that gives us an excessive *rush* (the exhilarating or calming feeling we get when we indulge in certain behaviors or drugs), we get into self-defeating behaviors that keep the rush coming (codependency). All rushes involve a change of mood. Examples include:

Chemical	Behavior	Produces
dopamine	running	excitement
	gambling	excitement
	hang gliding	excitement
serotonin	overeating	calm-comfort
	relationship dependency	comfort
norepinephrine	workaholism	power-control
	compulsive caretaking	power-control

These are only a few examples. There are many chemicals and behaviors currently being studied. For example, one of the major thrusts of the National Institutes of Health Research Grants is brain studies of compulsive overeating and its counterpart, anorexia. Research is also ongoing in the areas of compulsive and repetitive behaviors and sexual addiction as well.

It is important to know that we manipulate our moods— our highs and our lows—by our ingestion of chemicals from the outside (alcohol, drugs, nicotine, sugar, etc.). We do the same thing when we engage in selected, repetitive behaviors that release our inner chemicals. The behaviors listed earlier, such as workaholism and overeating, are the *result* of having the disease of codependency, not the *cause*.

With this knowledge, patients, staff, and those who are referred to treatment programs all understand codependency treatment. The primary focus of treatment is to address the person's brain processes (distorted thoughts, feelings, and behaviors), while the focus of aftercare is to address the issues in the person's life—such as low self-worth, difficult relationships, and medical problems—that have been affected by the brain disease. Knowing such specifics in treating codependency has helped us in many ways and has forced us to develop new tools and better methods in confronting denial, arresting compulsion, and creating an atmosphere that will allow our patients the most freedom to access their emotional lives.

Using traditional modalities of group dynamics, Gestalt psychology, psychodrama, and rage reduction, we have added formalized individual and group sculptures to specifically address codependency issues. These experiential methods are interwoven with 12-step programs, brain education, relationship exercises, and so on. Our book *Experiential Therapy for Co-Dependency Manual* (1991) was designed to train therapists in this style of treatment.

The Codependency Trap

When we can no longer attach what we feel to the event that caused it, we have a kind of free-floating depression or anxiety. There is a sense of discomfort, a sense of uneasiness inside. Some describe it as a panic in the chest. Others describe it as a literal pain in their stomachs. Some just feel like the end is coming, that they or the world is going to fall apart, and they have a sense of impending doom.

The emotional abscess is growing and the chronic pain becomes tiresome. When we find a medicating substance or behavior that helps alleviate the pain, it works through the *ventral tegmentum* (Bozarth 1987), an area in the brain having to do with reward and relief. Our emotions are signaling for help: "I need reward," "I need relief," "I need to change my internal environment," "I need to *feel* better." Many substances and many compulsive behaviors trigger our reward/relief/novelty center for temporary easing of discomfort.

We each seek those particular compulsive medicators that work best for us. Based on our genetic makeup, environmental learnings, present circumstances, and the amount and newness of the relief or reward, compulsive medicators are used with increasing frequency, duration, intensity, and variety. These increases are necessary because we quickly develop a tolerance to our medicators and need ever-increasing doses of frequency, duration, intensity, and variety for them to remain effective. Usually it's the excessive use of our medicators that causes the disability that results from our codependency. While those who become alcoholic or chemically dependent may have a certain genetic makeup that makes them susceptible to addiction, they also have an underlying craving for reward, relief, or novelty, all of which temporarily decrease their emotional pain.

Components Present
for Chemical Dependency

There are three components to chemical dependency:

1. Genes that result in a person being susceptible.

2. An agent that can cause the disease, such as alcohol or drugs.

3. A permissive or even promotive environment or society for the person and the agent to get together.

Perhaps the alcoholism in your family is three generations back; perhaps it was the last generation. Either way, you can have a genetic tendency toward chemical dependency. About 10 to 20 percent of adults in the United States have genes that make them inclined toward a particular kind of chemical relief from "outside" chemicals. Many people experiment with and overuse and misuse drugs and alcohol. For 10 to 20 percent of the population, drugs and alcohol provide some degree of special relief for the pain of an emotional abscess.

The chemicals that work on our brains from the outside include certain legal and illegal drugs—alcohol, nicotine, and perhaps caffeine and sugar. Among the chemicals that work from the outside, there are distinct differences. Nicotine, for example, is so reinforcing and works so quickly and subtly that anyone can become nicotine addicted and stay addicted for years and years, even after he or she stops smoking. On the other hand, research has shown that an individual has to have the proper genetic makeup before he or she will become addicted to alcohol (Ashton 1987). As yet, we don't know how sugar addiction occurs. It may be like alcohol addiction in that people are genetically predisposed to become addicted, but we do know that, for some people, sugar is an addictive, mood-changing substance.

So it appears that only certain people are likely to become addicted to alcohol and certain drugs, but it is possible for anyone to become addicted to nicotine and other kinds of drugs. Drugs, alcohol, nicotine, caffeine, and sugar have varying powers to quiet the craving that is triggered by emotional pain, but all are effective to some degree or another.

Behavioral Addiction

What happens to the 80 to 90 percent of the population who don't have the genes that make such outside chemicals, such as alcohol, work? If they have lived in painful kinds of situations, and if they have developed similar kinds of emotional abscesses, how do they cope? What we are now learning about the chemistry of the brain is helpful in understanding the answer to this question.

Today we know that we can become intoxicated and toxic with our own internal chemicals, which have been set off by behavior. We know we can also become "addicts" to and through our own behavior and that this can set off certain chemicals that satisfy our cravings for relief. The medicating behaviors that we see most often are:

- Workaholism
- Compulsive eating, which is different from sugar addiction
- Compulsive controlling of eating, such as anorexia, a highly medicating behavior
- Compulsive caretaking and controlling others
- Seduction
- Sexual acting out
- Spending and gambling
- Excessive exercise
- "Guru chasing"

"Guru chasing" is seen in adult children who are trying to recover from issues and are continually medicating these issues by chasing the newest "it," following the latest method of recovery, going to four or more different kinds of groups, going to numerous conferences, reading all the books and getting all the tapes, and trying to find something that is going to fix them and take care of them once and for all.

This chasing only temporarily medicates issues and pain. For example, consider the adult child from an alcoholic family who compulsively keeps trying to get better and better and who says, "I've been doing it all for two years and nothing's any better!" In fact, all they've been doing is medicating themselves but not opening up and working through the emotional abscess.

Internal chemicals that are stimulated by compulsive behaviors, or outside chemicals taken internally, will temporarily quiet an emotional abscess, but then both kinds of medicators require repeating with increasing frequency, duration, amount, and variety to overcome tolerance. In this way, individuals become addicted to or dependent on their behaviors or substances, or a combination of behaviors or substances. Certainly it's a rare individual who is only a workaholic or an alcoholic, or who is only a nicotine addict or only has an eating disorder. Scratch the surface paint off a substance abuser and you'll find a "behavioral" abuser. Most individuals have many coexisting dependencies.

Certainly it's a rare individual who is
only a workaholic or an alcoholic, or who is only
a nicotine addict or only has an eating disorder.
Scratch the surface paint off a substance
abuser and you'll find a "behavioral" abuser.
Most individuals have many
coexisting dependencies.

The result of medicating is called a "high." Whether it comes in a package of novelty, reward, or relief, it's still a high. And what happens after every high? You crash. And you say to yourself:

Damn it, I did it again! I didn't mean to.

This time I meant to really, really manage the way I work in my job.

This time I really, really meant to abstain, be honest, committed, and faithful.

This time I really, really meant to just live some sort of a simple life for a while, and I found myself signing up for three more workshops.

I didn't mean to eat that Twinkie.

I didn't mean to have another drink.

I didn't intend to have a cigarette on the way home from the program.

This is negative reinforcement, and it's filled with disgust. We don't like ourselves, and we reinforce our own shame as our self-worth plummets and our abscesses grow. There comes a time when we need to say, "I'm finished with it!" There comes a time when it is obvious that we must get rid of all our feelings about our emotional abscess. That's what treatment is for—to get rid of it; to work *through* the abscess, not make it worse.

Many people who are still struggling have worked on the same issues fifteen times or more. "I want to keep working on this issue," they say, or "I found one more piece of this issue." Such head talk is making a commitment to shame and to staying in the pathology rather than going through it, letting it go, and making a commitment not to return to the same issue. We reinforce our shame when we go back and drag ourselves through it one more time. Sometimes, in a way, it's easier than recovery.

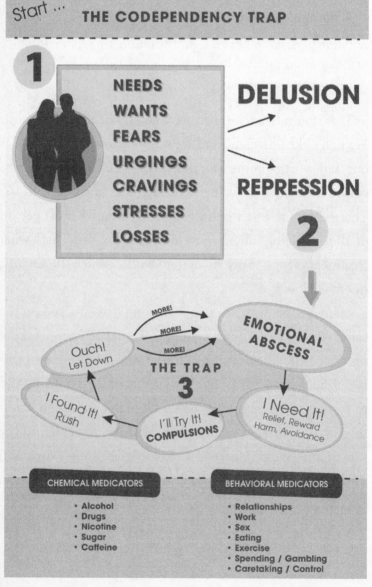

Figure 2.1. Codependency: Reinforcement Theory

When you recover, you have a lot of new responsibilities and many things to do. Intimacy is possible, but now there are also new possibilities for failure because there are so many options open to you. Many people are really afraid to recover, and this is why they keep finding one more problem to work on. Familiar pain can be comfortable and a means of bonding with people and obtaining acceptance. Misery loves company. Okay, so we crashed and we feel disgusted with ourselves. We feel guilty once more. And many of us feel just plain stupid. We feed the emotional abscess, and the bigger it gets, the more relief we crave.

Just as we develop a tolerance to the effects of chemicals, we develop a tolerance to the effects of our behaviors. Now we don't need just one promotion, we need two promotions—and they've got to be bigger. It isn't just about getting a raise but getting a big raise and some public recognitions. For the person who is acting out, it's got to be more (frequency) and more (duration) and more (variety) and more (intensity) to overcome tolerance. This is the whole trap of codependency. This vicious one-way circle is a trap that ends in depression, isolation, institutions, and sometimes death.

CHAPTER 3

Personality and the Progression into Disease

I n her book entitled *Another Chance: Hope and Help for the Alcoholic Family*, Sharon Wegscheider-Cruse described four roles within dysfunctional families that provide distinct functions within the family unit. They include the Family Hero, the Scapegoat, the Lost Child, the Enabler, and the Mascot. Let's look at these self-defeating behaviors in more detail.

Family Hero

The Family Hero provides the moments of hope and pride that the family desperately needs. The hero tries to bring self-worth to the family by excelling in various fields, such as sports, music, academics, art, military service, and so on. The hero is often an award winner in his or her chosen field, which brings reflected notoriety to the family. To the outside world the hero looks great, but on the inside the hero feels miserable. Inadequacy, loneliness, and fatigue contribute to feelings of worthlessness and of being overwhelmed.

Scapegoat

Scapegoats, aware of the dysfunction surrounding them, try to spend more and more time away from the family, yet take with them a hunger for belonging and anger because they do not belong at home. This need for belonging and the pain of anger often leads the Scapegoat to dysfunctional peer groups and experimentation with chemicals. Chemical dependency, negative behavior, and suicide are often escapes for the Scapegoat. Since Scapegoats frequently draw negative attention to themselves by getting into trouble at school or with the law, the family often pins its collective dysfunction onto the Scapegoat, who bears the burden at a cost to himself or herself.

Lost Child

The Lost Child adapts. She becomes a loner who tries to survive her painful environment. In the midst of family chaos, the Lost Child withdraws into himself. This child is often forgotten to the degree that he or she is neglected by the family. As these children build walls of isolation, they miss out on how to develop relationships. They suffer from intense loneliness.

Enablers

The Enabler is frequently a parent or a spouse in a dysfunctional family. The Enabler is driven by anger and disappointment. Things are not turning out the way that was expected. Covering up problems and controlling the behaviors of the other family members is a 24/7 job for the Enabler who assumes the role of providing a picture of the perfect family to the community. Enablers are powerless and self-righteous and can end up as disillusioned martyrs.

Mascots

Mascots are filled with fear (of being left out) and loneliness (they are rarely taken seriously by the family). To try to become included, mascots turn to teasing, joking, or any agitating behavior to attract attention to themselves. Mascots may act cute or helpless and interrupt or act "crazy;" they are very hard to ignore.

Since these roles were first delineated, they have proven to be useful to both the layperson and also to professionals who work with alcoholic families. Over the years, the roles have become ingrained in treatment with all painful families, not just the alcoholic family. Many therapists and schools and treatment programs have developed their approach to helping families by using these four roles. The film *The Family Trap*, which gives Sharon's philosophy about the roles, has become a classic in treatment programs.

However, many in the scientific community, while recognizing the value of the roles, wanted to know why they were so accurate and how identifying with them helped an individual. These questions remained unanswered until the work of C. Robert Cloninger became known. In 1987, Cloninger proposed that there were three dimensions of the personality that could be seen in chemically dependent individuals. This three-dimensional model of personality, which became known as the "tridimensional theory of personality," is still widely used today, and we have found that these same dimensions can be clearly seen in many codependents. These dimensions are (1) reward dependence; (2) novelty seeking; and (3) harm avoidance.

Those with reward dependence, as the name implies, seek rewards and are always ready to "grab for the ring" or prize. They constantly control their environment in an attempt to maintain the status quo. Their self-worth depends on accomplishment, position, possessions (including people), and power. This trait is exemplified by workaholics. As reward dependents, they frenetically seek the pat on the back. They need to have the approval of others.

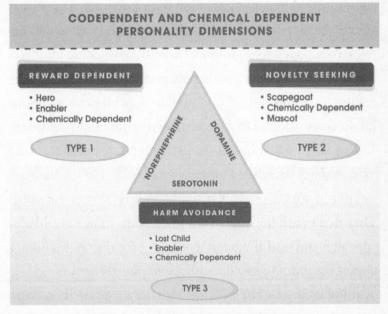

Figure 3.1. Inherited Personality Dimensions
(Cloninger modified)

Novelty seekers are the kind of people who seek excitement and are never satisfied. Novelty seekers like to live with crisis and adventure. Over the past fifteen years, interest in the genetic and brain aspects of novelty seeking or thrill seeking has grown. For example, a 1996 *Los Angeles Times* Wire Services article revealed that: "One specific kind of genetic variation makes people more likely to be excitable, fickle, thrill seeking and quick-tempered, according to two studies published today. If confirmed by further research, that association would be among the first found between a gene that affects brain chemistry and a normal aspect of personality.

"Two independent groups of scientists, working in different countries and using different methods, report the same results in *Nature Genetics*: Individuals who have a certain kind of extra-long DNA sequence on part of chromosome 11 also score much higher on psychological tests measuring a personality trait called 'novelty seeking.'"

Those with harm avoidance like to keep things the same. They don't rock the boat. They like things to be easy, like to appear normal to the outside world, take no risks, and are always on guard to avoid conflict and punishment.

All of us have some of these inherited traits. When these traits work for us, they grow into balanced, mature, and flexible behaviors that we can use, but when our normal personality patterns are exaggerated, problems can arise that lead to disorders. For example, the person who seeks excitement and drama is never satisfied, lives on the edge, and becomes preoccupied with self as a means of coping with stress, and emotional pain crosses a fine line from balanced and flexible novelty-seeking to exaggerated novelty-seeking.

Learning about these three dimensions of personality helped us to further understand the family roles described earlier. The novelty seeker can become a clinical narcissist, a borderline personality, or a histrionic. As a child, this type of person might be the family Scapegoat or Mascot. The exaggerated harm avoidant tends to become the Lost Child and is likely to become clinically diagnosed with an avoidant personality disorder, which at times may progress to a schizoid (isolated) personality disorder. He or she may also be clinically depressed. The reward dependent person becomes obsessive-compulsive or passive-aggressive. In the family this person is often the Family Hero.

What continually reinforces each personality pattern is the release of relief or reward brain chemicals. The Mascot and the Scapegoat in the family are often novelty seekers. The Family Hero, the Enabler, and the Lost Child are quite likely to marry alcoholics. When a harm-avoidant person marries an alcoholic, he or she is likely marrying a novelty seeker, because these two play off of each other's pathologies.

Novelty seekers often get "high" on their own internal chemicals with an effect that is similar to that produced by alcohol or drugs. When they take risks, make sudden changes, and create crises over and over again, their brains release dopamine, a brain chemical used to transmit "high" messages throughout our bodies. Reward-dependent workaholics are probably releasing their own norepinephrine (adrenaline). Good workaholics are probably releasing both norepinephrine and dopamine. They're staying as medicated as a person smoking dope. Harm-avoidant individuals who go to their rooms and hide out watching TV, eating potato chips, and purging are releasing their own serotonin, a built-in tranquilizer we all have.

This information helps us understand the four roles in families and why they are so important. But does this then mean that everyone is or could be codependent? *Not at all!* Codependency represents a collection of disabling compulsions accompanied by delusion and emotional repression and is the first step in the progression from health to disease. This first step occurs when we cross a line from balanced and flexible traits and dimensions to rigid and exaggerated traits and dimensions. There is a point where we progress from the normal personality traits we all have and exaggerate those traits into a rigid, self-defeating pattern.

The work of Theodore Millon (1985–87) suggests that the inherited aspects of our personalities are influenced by prenatal and natal factors to which are added experiences and knowledge as we grow. Theoretically, we should all be able to acquire a normal personality that helps us face adversity and that recovers time and time again.

What Is Mental Illness?

Millon and others believe that mental illnesses are deviations from normal personality traits. Exaggeration of one set of traits gives rise to one type of personality disorder or mental illness, while exaggeration of another set of traits results in another type of mental illness or personality disorder. Others think that mental illnesses are each distinct and believe that an outside process has intruded upon a person's thinking, feeling, and behaving. (This view is certainly correct for certain infections that cause mental confusion, impulsive behavior, etc.)

We believe that codependency is an exaggeration of normal personality traits to the degree that a person becomes disabled (disease of codependency). Although Millon suggests that personality disorders result from exaggerated personality traits, we see codependency as a "pre-personality disorder." The difference we see thus far is a matter of degree and reversibility. Codependency does not seem to be as restricting or ingrained as are actual personality disorders.

Codependency can be as severe and disabling as personality disorders, but codependents seem to have more recovery resources and choices available to them, whether they know it or not. Many times our treatment succeeds with people primarily by showing them that they have such choices and resources. People with personality disorders seem to have less access to resources and choices that could help them. They require much more therapeutic effort to reverse their disorders, and many cannot be reversed.

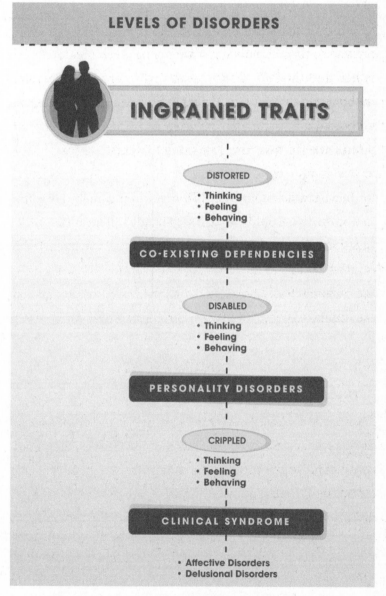

Figure 3.2. Advancing Stages of Personality Pathology

CHAPTER 4

Symptoms of Codependency: Brain Events

It helps to describe Brain Events by their most prominent characteristics: denial/delusion, emotional repression, and compulsion. These Brain Events, sometimes called mental mechanisms or defenses (which we refer to as symptoms throughout this chapter), can be helpful to us if used in moderation and in the proper situation. It is when they are severely exaggerated in their intensity, frequency of use, and improper use that they lead to disruptions in our lives.

Symptoms Group One: Denial/Delusion (Distorted Thinking)

Denial is the failure to acknowledge an unacceptable truth or emotion or to admit it into consciousness; it is used as a defense mechanism. Because of denial, codependents cannot admit that their codependent thinking and behavior is causing any problems. The way they think and behave brings them relief and they are not about to give that up. These kinds of thoughts require a large amount of denial of the truth and of reality. Because of "euphoric recall," they easily remember the good times and forget the bad times. This is called "nicotine nostalgia" for smokers or "cool happenings" for codependents and serves as an additional stimulus to continue.

A codependent must do a lot of dimming of their usually helpful "reality pathways." They must minimize, deny, forget, and debunk any knowledge or awareness they have. They dim and shut down what they know to be true; they will need to suppress the feelings that come with being unable to stop their behaviors and the feelings they get from ignoring the worries of their spouses, children, other family members, and friends. Codependents are very adept at dimming their reality pathways, knowledge pathways, and values pathways. It keeps them in denial and allows them to justify their behavior.

> Most people would learn from their mistakes if they weren't so busy denying them.
>
> —Harold J. Smith

Alcoholism Denial

Hans was an alcoholic. He had severe cirrhosis of the liver; he was yellow and short of breath on his last admission to the hospital. He was asked if he drank too much alcohol. He struggled to open his eyes, frowned, and slowly shook his head from side to side. He died as the ultimate example of denial.

Codependent Denial

Codependent denial can be much more subtle and even creative. One of the ways individuals can avoid looking too closely at their own difficulties is to deny they exist. For example, if we "believe" we have been given a special capability to always be there for others and we indulge in that 150 percent, whether we really want to or not, it helps us to deny there is a need for us to look at our own opinions of ourselves and our past and present way of living.

Marilyn gained most of her feeling of self-respect from her membership in her club. She had waited a long time to be elected as social chairman. She was early for every meeting, was first to volunteer for any task, talked of nothing else at home, and was totally preoccupied about her next "move" to gain recognition. She certainly did not recognize her behavior as a "move." She insisted that the next meeting would be a potluck affair. She would make two of her special casseroles so she could leave one at home for her husband and the girls. She would call from the meeting to remind him when to put the dish in the oven, at what temperature, for how long, where the salad was in the refrigerator, and which dressing to use. She would need to hurry the phone call so she could start her forty-five-minute PowerPoint presentation at the meeting on time. She would skip eating. The entire family suffered when she was not elected to any other position in the club. She had to believe she was in the club for the club's benefit and not her own ego massage. They tried to explain this to her in the gentlest terms, but she vigorously denied all of their suggestions.

More Codependent Denial

Also, concentrating our lives and interest in areas where there is "built-in praise" can be very damaging to a person's life. Built-in praise allows us to deny that anything is wrong, that we are not successful, special, and so on. It is easy in this culture of intense marketing, advertising, and communication for individuals to become dependent on built-in praise and to be totally focused on who they know, where they work, and where they live. What they have, the cars they drive, the parties they give, the clothes they wear—all are extremely important. All this and more can make them feel "special." "How could anything be wrong? Look what I have and have done!"

Delusion

Delusion occurs when we unconsciously change reality or our reality becomes distorted because we do not use all the information available to us. Usually preceded by denial, either of events or of feelings, it leads to a distortion of our beliefs about the way the world or our families are. We live with our own narrow view of what we see and how we see it. We disavow reality.

Overall this symptom of codependency can be characterized as showing distorted thinking on the part of the individual.

In unhealthy families, people are taught either directly or indirectly not to be honest with all they see, hear, and feel. They begin to learn in their painful family how to separate themselves from the total view and live with a limited view.

Many of us, in different ways, have dissociated from how it really was and have chosen to believe how we want it to have been. When we dissociate from the reality of what we truly feel, we are being dishonest with ourselves. This leads to distorted thinking, including lying to yourself and to others about the pain you're in. It means that you do not experience the whole picture.

Dissociation

An example of cognitive, affective, behavioral dissociation was given by a patient whose father would come into her bedroom at night and sexually molest her from the time that she was about nine to fourteen years old. To this day, she sleeps with her hands in a ball because she said that she learned that when he would come in drunk at night, she would just lie as still yet taut as she could and feel her fingernails digging into her hands. She dissociated by saying, "This is not happening to me," while he sexually molested her.

Her mind (cognitive) said, "This is not happening to me." Her feelings (affective) went numb. Her action (behavioral) was to concentrate on the pain of digging her fingernails into her palms.

Peter Alsop wrote a song called "Look at the Ceiling." It's a little girl's story of making up fairy tales about the shadows on the ceiling of her bedroom while her father molests her. It's much too painful for her to be aware of what is happening, so she creates a fantasy filled with pleasant thoughts. Later on in life she uses the mechanism of dissociation to leave unpleasant situations. This impairs her view of reality.

Dissociation is what happens to the young man whose father said, "Come on, knucklehead, shape up. What kind of a man are you going to grow up to be if you cry?" From this kind of remark the little boy learns to dissociate from his shame, hurt, guilt, and anger. He's living in an environment where he is simply neither rewarded nor acknowledged for feeling feelings. This little boy also learns to create a "fantasy reality" to escape to whenever he is in emotional pain.

As we begin to dissociate, we become deluded about our reality and lose sight of the truth. So a big part of delusion is dissociation, the separation of oneself from how it is. All of this adds up to distorted thinking so that, as adults, we're not sure how everything was. Many of us remember the past as being better than it was because we like to have happy memories.

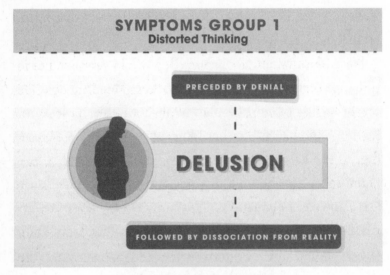

Figure 4.1. Symptoms Group One
(Distorted Thinking): Delusion

Symptoms Group Two (Distorted Feelings): Emotional Repression

Emotional repression occurs when we suppress a thought, feeling, or desire so that it becomes or remains unconscious. The metaphor of an emotional abscess is very descriptive of an abscess of suppressed feelings. An actual abscess cannot be reached well with antibiotics; it is too sealed off in the body. It needs surgery to open it and drain its contents. It cannot be sewn closed after it is opened because it will just form into another abscess. Its healing time is slow; it needs to heal from the inside to the outside, there is discomfort from it, and it leaves a scar.

An emotional abscess, composed of old repressed emotions, cannot be reached by mood-altering medications. This would be like using pain medications to treat an abscess; the pain may be alleviated for a while, but the true problem hasn't been dealt with. Medications cannot cure the actual abscess, although they might be quite helpful for a time in the management of it. The emotional abscess needs to be opened up by therapeutic techniques and drained of its repressed contents by reexperiencing the original feelings and then releasing them through emotional cleansing (catharsis). This process has a slow healing time, because the abscess needs to heal from the "inside out," and it has its own discomfort and may leave a scar. But just as with an actual scar, the tenderness and deep colors recede. After time, the scar is hardly noticeable and pain free.

Jerry's income tax form listed him as head of the household, and he took it seriously. When he got home from work and emotions were flying all over the house, he would take charge. His sense of responsibility to settle the fray was greater than his feeling of empathy for his young child, who was, perhaps in the wrong, being truly hurt. He suppressed his feelings for the members of his family in order to be the minister of justice. He had no clue that he could teach and share feelings simultaneously.

Jerry's job was to watch everyone else cry, but not cry himself. Family rules were passed to him, and he saw no harm in passing these same rules on down. He took pride in being very slow to show anger, if at all. His fears were an abomination to him, and he was always busy suppressing them while he was still in school. They were even more threatening to his adult self. He had to push his fears down if he was to be a good head of the household. His ulcers perforated twice in three years.

Each time we dissociate from reality and deny what is happening, we repress or stuff the feelings that go with the event. Shutting down those feelings leads to a condition of emotional repression. After a while those various feelings that one shuts down become mixed together like a stew. This emotional mixture is called *undifferentiated emotion*. This means that we don't even know what we feel anymore or what the feeling represents. Is it anger, guilt, hurt, or shame? What is it? The events also get lost. First of all, we deny the events, and then over time the events and feelings get lost, causing us to experience free-floating feelings, such as free-floating anxiety (an emotion without any apparent cause) or free-floating anger. It is undifferentiated emotion that churns inside, giving us deep, chronic emotional pain.

It is important for us to acknowledge that it is our emotional pain that causes our craving for relief. We crave some kind of relief from what we feel, even though we don't know which feeling we feel. This craving triggers compulsions (substances and behaviors) that give us temporary relief. A vicious cycle is set in motion. (This cycle is described in Chapter 2, "The Codependency Trap.")

The first stage of dependency is to seek some sort of change of mood that is pleasurable, rewarding, or relief-producing to deal with this craving for relief. Both mood-altering substances and mood-altering behaviors can provide feelings of reward or relief. Different substances and behaviors work for different people.

Some find that one or more of the predictable mood-changing substances, such as alcohol, are effective in producing relief. Mood-altering chemicals provide temporary relief from deeply buried inner pain, but for those who are genetically set up to react to such mood-changing chemicals, dependency and addiction will begin.

Emotions

Because the healing of our emotional pain is at the core of recovery from codependency, we need to share our concept that our emotions are a major part of our sixth sense. What we call our intuition is a perception based upon our current observations, past experiences, our memories and knowledge, and our ability to analyze and come to a conclusion. Intuition's *power* comes through the emotions generated by those components of intuition. We often describe our intuition as "I have a gut feeling about that . . ." Repressed emotions slip out in sarcasm, arrogance, irritability, a need to control, and isolation. In therapy, we actually have to reexperience the pain in order to release old emotional abscesses.

Example of an Emotional Abscess

When there is old rage and anger boiling up deep inside, it becomes necessary for the person to reexperience that old anger and rage in order to release it. Healing follows release. There are specific therapy models that have been designed to do just that. To heal all feelings, anger, grief, hurt, and so on, there needs to be some degree of reexperiencing and release.

This isn't to say that we'll never have painful feelings again, but the goal of recovery is to (1) acknowledge the feelings and allow ourselves to fully feel them; and then (2) let go of them. Some people ask, "If I get rid of all my anger, hurt, and rage, does that mean that I'll never have to be angry, hurt, or rageful again?" The answer is no. All it means is that with proper help, we have the opportunity to reexperience (incise) and get rid of (drain) the emotional abscess that keeps us stuck in today's unhappy life.

Because an emotion is a biochemical action and reaction, emotions have two lives, two senses of energy. When you feel an emotion—which is a message coming from your sensory system—the message says, "React to me, respond to me, do something." For example, if your sensory system says, "I'm scared," then what you feel is fear and what you might do is run. If your sensory system says to you, "I'm feeling sensual and I'm feeling love and excitement," what you do is express that emotion verbally and nonverbally by responding and by becoming aroused.

> Our feelings are a sensory system—
> something to which we respond.

We respond to our sense of touch when we pull back from a hot stove or repeatedly stroke a soft piece of velvet or another person. We respond to our sense of smell when we leave a place to avoid noxious fumes or when we sample fragrances before purchasing them. We respond to our sense of sight when we duck from a flying object or linger over a sunset or a piece of art. We respond to our sense of hearing when we turn our heads and move our bodies to avoid a blast or we listen to nature or replay a pleasant piece of music. We respond to our sense of taste when we spit out bitter or tainted food or when we suck a mint or savor a special sauce.

These five physical senses are interwoven with learning, memory, and emotions. Our emotions may be our sixth sense and possibly our closest link to reality. They need to be responded to every bit as much as our other five senses.

Receiving Chemical Messages

One can become accustomed to an emotional abscess even while it's growing. Repression becomes so efficient that one's emotions appear to have shrunk or disappeared. It's difficult to ascertain if certain people are happy, sad, or excited. They seem to have low energy and no expression. Their feelings are so piled on top of one another, so intertwined, that you can't get any kind of message from them whatsoever. The feeling that usually rises to the top like cream in milk, however, is anger.

When you get really, really close to someone who has a lot of unexpressed anger, when you get close to his or her space, you can feel it. You can feel his or her vibrations. Have you ever felt that with somebody? What they are doing is giving you chemical messages that are saying, "I'm chuck up to here with old feelings I've never dealt with and my anger is sitting right on my shoulder." The old chip on the shoulder. You can feel vibrations from an angry person; they spill out.

You can also learn to feel welcoming messages. You can

learn to read a lot of different kinds of messages, depending on what people have been giving you or not giving you emotionally. In essence, recovery is getting rid of the old abscess of emotional repression so that you can experience your precious feeling life.

How many parents have ever said to their kids, "Boy, you got an A in math. That's fantastic. You got an A- in science, terrific! You got an A in expressing your feelings! That's really good!" Not many, if any.

The more we've discovered about our emotions—such as where certain emotions are processed in the brain, how various hormones affect us emotionally, and so on—the better equipped we are to understand how they work in our lives. Just as we learn to touch, see, smell, hear, and taste, and respond to those sensations, we can also learn to feel our emotions and respond to them. A lot of people are walking around emotionally disabled and in pain because they don't know how to do this.

When codependents struggle with distorted reality, emotional repression occurs. When we do not express what we feel, we repress. Because feelings are a part of everyday life, the distortion of events and emotions occur simultaneously. If we don't allow ourselves to cry, be angry, grieve, and be vulnerable, then we carry a painful emotional load around that is composed of all those old angers and irritations.

If you never had the opportunity to express your anger and pain when you felt it as a child and during your growing-up years, then you probably still carry that rage today. Many of us have carried a ton of rage with us for a long time! We relieve ourselves of the load from time to time by different means, some of which are damaging to ourselves and our relationships with others.

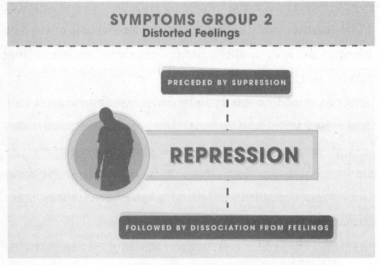

SYMPTOMS GROUP 2
Distorted Feelings

PRECEDED BY SUPRESSION

REPRESSION

FOLLOWED BY DISSOCIATION FROM FEELINGS

Figure 4.2. Symptoms Group Two (Distorted Feelings): Emotional Repression

Symptoms Group Three:
Compulsions (Distorted Behavior)

A compulsion is an irresistible urge to behave in a certain way, especially against one's conscious wishes. Approval seeking by association with "the right people" at any cost to oneself is a common compulsive behavior for codependents. The right people might be a clique of people, a certain girlfriend or boyfriend, or people who hold a high office or high position in our judgment. One becomes a hanger-on because the reward and relief is considered such a driving force.

To be in control is soothing and consoling for wounded feelings or feelings of guilt and shame. Excitement seeking and exciting behavior, as well as alcohol, drugs, and prescription medications, are also soothing for those with compulsive behaviors. Compulsive behaviors often evolve into addictive behaviors.

Over the years, for children from painful homes, there has been an inner cesspool or emotional abscess of shame, hurt, loneliness, anger, inadequacy, sadness, and hopelessness. It is deep inside and kept locked away. It hurts, and the need for relief from the pain becomes a craving. Compulsive use of substances and behaviors medicates the emotional abscess for a while.

The body can become physically dependent on mood-altering chemicals. This is well-known as addiction to chemicals or chemical dependency. But the body can also become physically dependent on certain behaviors. So compulsions to use substances *and/or* behavior become the armament of the codependent.

Diane had grown up in an alcoholic home. Her dad had become an alcoholic, and she believed her mom had "allowed" it. She promised herself she would not have that happen to her. Her mother just didn't know how to handle her father's drinking. She knew she was on her own: her 4.0 GPA and practically running the house didn't help the situation at all.

She worked hard because it made her feel better, and she received much praise for her efforts. She met an alcoholic who wasn't currently drinking and fell in love. But this was different. He had gone five years without a drink and had a great business going. She took things into her own hands and took on the job of keeping him sober. She abstained from drinking any alcohol herself, disallowed any alcohol in the house, accepted invitations only to events where alcohol was not prominent, and insisted that her husband use numerous dietary supplements for alcoholics that she had read about. She always traveled with him. She dreaded his retirement.

Diane demonstrates the Brain Events of codependency perfectly. She felt she needed to keep him busy so he would never drink again. She took over ownership of his abstinence and well-being. That is true codependence.

Crutches of Compulsion

Mood-altering chemicals provide relief from deeply buried inner pain. It is a temporary relief, but for those whose bodies react addictively, it is a potent one that works almost every time. Drugs and alcohol are effective pain relievers. So is nicotine.

Smoking interferes with the attainment of intimacy and personal growth and serves as a security blanket or insulator from the world of uncertainty and psychic pain. By turning to cigarettes during times of stress, people are less likely to find strength within themselves. In a sense, for many people, including many recovering drug and alcohol addicts, tobacco is held on to as that one last crutch.

> Smoking interferes with the attainment of intimacy and personal growth and serves as a security blanket or insulator from the world of uncertainty and psychic pain.

Crutches are interesting. When a leg is broken, crutches help you get around. But after the leg has mended, it is vital that the crutches be put back into the closet, otherwise the leg's muscle will shrivel from disuse and eventually become so weak and withered as to become truly useless—and render the user chronically in need of a crutch.

So many people have withered emotional muscles. For whatever reason, at some point in our lives we decided to lean upon a drink, some other drug, a cigarette, an unhealthy relationship, or something else in order to help deal with emotional discomfort—and it worked for a while. Unfortunately, long after the precipitating events that made smoking or whatever seem so attractive had passed, the crutch remained . . . and remained and remained. Meanwhile, the emotional muscle deteriorated beyond its original fragile condition, further increasing dependence upon the crutch.

There are a variety of crutches and relief-producing behaviors. Some rushes and some types of relief last ten minutes, some last twenty, and some last up to an hour, but they all have one thing in common: as you use them, you begin to anticipate some kind of rush or relief from the anxiety and pain you feel.

Not everybody is able to get that special kind of relief from alcohol and drugs, because some people do not have the genetic makeup for it. There are many people who have painful lives and who crave relief, but alcohol and drugs are not their answer. They are not any better or any different from drug addicts or alcoholics, just genetically programmed differently. These people find other means, depending on their circumstances, their family system, or on what works for them. Some people are set up to be sugar sensitive, and sugar does for them what alcohol does not.

Control Crutches

For families that are very perfectionistic, stoic, and cognitive, people are set up to get a rush through the power of control. In stoic and perfectionistic families, we find the anorexic, the person who starves and gets a rush from controlling intake and attention, as well as having a drive to obtain the "perfect" body. Some get good feelings from compulsive overeating. Some actually feel a temporary rush and then calmness from purging. Eating disorders are chronic, progressive, and sometimes fatal diseases if left untreated.

> Eating disorders are chronic, progressive, and sometimes fatal diseases if left untreated.

Anorexia nervosa is a relentless pursuit of thinness, which may be characterized by self-starvation, compulsive exercise, and laxative abuse. *Bulimia* is the addictive binge/purge cycle, which is characterized by compulsively eating and then purging by self-induced vomiting or laxative and diuretic abuse.

In cognitive, perfectionistic families, we also find those who are addicted to the workaholic rush. These people maintain a certain tolerable level of their internal pain by staying frenetically active and involved. They go from one thing to another thing, accomplishing great things—or nothing at all.

> In cognitive, perfectionistic families, we also find those who are addicted to the workaholic rush. These people maintain a certain tolerable level of their internal pain by staying frenetically active.

People can get a rush in a variety of ways. People can rush with what we call "green-paper" addiction, which covers the whole realm of how people spend money. This includes occasional overspending to living on credit cards and never really believing you have to pay them off. Green-paper addiction includes gambling, which is one of the toughest of the compulsions to treat. The seduction of gambling tends to be a tremendous codependency issue.

So drugs, alcohol, nicotine, and for some, sugar and caffeine are major chemical medicators of emotional pain. They are the most common chemical substances with which we see people form toxic relationships. Workaholism, overeating, purging and not eating, sexual acting out, relationship and sex dependency, controlling and compulsive caretaking, as well as spending and gambling, are the most common behavioral medicators that codependents learn to use for the pain of their emotional abscess.

Intimacy Crutches

Sexuality lends itself very well as an example of a behavioral medicator or compulsion. There are many different ways to look at what happens to people who are struggling with sexual behavioral problems and sexual dysfunction. The good news is that we have learned that sexual acting out as a codependency compulsion is treatable.

Some become very dependent on and even skilled in the process of the seduction aspects of a relationship. This is because seduction contains a lot of feelings. Seduction is very emotional. You share feelings; you have this stirring inside because of the sharing of information and vulnerability.

For adult children or codependents who do not have feelings readily available to them, the kind of natural growing seduction that comes from a natural passion doesn't happen. Instead they may become trapped in a cycle of seduction, only getting their rush from the romantic beginnings of a new sexual relationship or conquest. When the excitement of the seduction phase of a relationship ends, they are not able to access their deeper feelings and move on to a genuinely passionate relationship. These people seem to be caught up in a cycle of love 'em and leave 'em.

The word *passion* means "full of feeling." When we enter into a close relationship, we quickly see that we need the ability to be full of feelings before we can experience intimacy with each other. Intimacy is the coming together of feelings and may or may not include sexual contact. A term for describing this coming together is *emotional intercourse*.

> When we enter into a close relationship, we quickly see that we need the ability to be full of feelings before we can experience intimacy with each other.

Too many adult children and codependents have settled for a passionless relationship because their feelings have been medicated by substances or behaviors—or both. This is not the same as a sexless relationship.

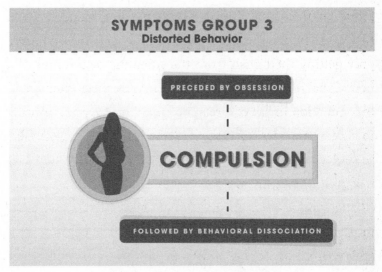

Figure 4.3. Symptoms Group Three
(Distorted Behavior): Compulsion

Passion has to do with waking up one's own life and becoming a passionate person. People who have chosen and learned how to do this become capable of intimacy and emotional intercourse. Treatment for a preexisting emotional abscess and waking up repressed feelings allows a person to act from a passion base and eliminates the need for a sexual behavior medicator in the form of sexual compulsions.

Summary

Whether the compulsive medicator is . . .

- Caretaking
- Refusing food
- Acting out sexually
- Workaholism
- Power/control
- Nicotine (physical addiction)
- Alcohol (physical addiction)
- Drugs (physical addiction)

. . . . the symptom groups of the basic disease of codependency are:

1. Denial/Delusion (distorted thinking)
2. Emotional repression (distorted feeling)
3. Compulsion (distorted behavior)

The word *distorted* indicates a deviation from normal, efficient, full, and flexible thinking, feeling, and behaving (Stone 1988). Indeed, the disorder of codependency appears to be a deviation from normal thinking, feeling, and behaving, which is an early part of a continuum from mental health to severe mental illness.

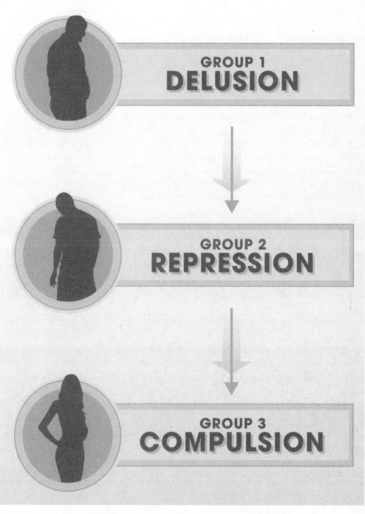

Figure 4.4. Summary of Brain Events

CHAPTER 5

Complications of Codependency: Life Events

Complications Group One: Low Self-Worth (Disabled Spirituality)

The first complication of codependency is chronic low self-worth, which is a condition of feeling shame. There is a difference between guilt and shame. *Guilt is felt when one does something to harm oneself or others.* The wonderful thing about guilt, and the reason guilt can be such a positive feeling, is that when we recognize it, we can make amends and then feel good about ourselves.

Guilt has a pattern that brings us back to feeling good if we pursue it. Every bit of guilt can be amended one way or another. So guilt is a very productive feeling. To begin to feel guilty in places where it's appropriate and then to begin to make amends is to be on a straight path to self-worth and healing. Guilt is the feeling of "I've done something bad and I would like to make amends about it and change."

> Guilt is a very productive feeling.
> To begin to feel guilty in places where it's appropriate and then begin to make amends is to be on a straight path to self-worth and healing.

Shame is feeling that you are what is bad. It is the belief that you are bad; not that you did something bad, but that you are inherently faulty. Dysfunctional families tend to produce shame-based people. In hurting families, people bring generations of shame into their current lives. What does not get resolved in the generation before comes as a package to the children. It's part of the cycle of shame.

Shame can be about:

- Affairs
- Alcoholism
- Anorexia
- Being overweight
- Bulimia
- Drug addiction

- Gambling
- Physical defects
- Poverty
- Sexual abuse
- Suicide
- Wealth

Figure 5.1. Complications Group 1: Low Self-Worth

It's what came with our package, and we feel ashamed about that.

Then when you add in all those old family messages, those inhumane rules, you end up with people who feel "less than" or unworthy. These people end up with chronic low self-worth, which is the state of being based on shame. When we are shame-based, it is difficult to make decisions on what we need for ourselves. People experience perceived powerlessness. They believe they are bad and unworthy and there is nothing they can do to change. Needless to say, this often creates a self-fulfilling prophecy.

Shame is probably the primary fuel that keeps the disease process of codependency running and causes relapses to occur. It is the result of a learned belief or state rather than the cause of codependency. Shame doesn't initiate codependency; it results from having the disease of codependency. Scratch the paint off of shame, and rage and anger come boiling through. Resolution of that rage and anger refertilizes self-worth and allows the true beauty of the individual to blossom forth.

Origins of Low Self-Worth

About every five years there is a current, popular new word for low self-worth. It's the kind of self-worth that isn't specific to an event, such as "I wish I were as good-looking as Verna"; "I wish I were as rich as Bill"; or "I wish I were as smart as Marilyn." It's the ongoing, constant state of low self-worth that invalidates our right to be. It's the self-worth that says, "I am a faulty person." And it's the self-worth that stays with us so long that we literally grow up believing that we don't even have the right to a full recovery or the right to make choices, changes, and decisions in our lives. We relinquish our right to be ourselves.

As we were growing up, many of us were not taught that we were valuable simply because we exist. That's all. That's why we are precious. We are alive and therefore we are of worth. Many of us believe that our only value is in being valuable to someone else: "I am my father's daughter"; "I am my husband's wife"; "I am my children's parent"; "I am my employer's employee"; and so on. The fact that we are of worth in and of ourselves hardly ever occurs to a person with low self-worth.

When low self-worth people do make decisions, they tend to make them lifetime decisions. People with low self-worth frequently make poor choices personally and professionally. They aren't aware or they can't believe that they can make new choices, that they don't have to stay stuck their entire lives. They become preoccupied with "other"-worth. They get their worth from others and not from themselves.

The hooks come from others' expectations of us. Hooks need to be removed for us to be free. We need to be detached from our two-way, unhealthy dependencies on our families of origin, our work, and even our spouses and children. Being detached doesn't mean desertion. Someone might say, "Well, that sounds pretty self-centered." This type of self-centeredness is more accurately defined as "a centered self."

A centered self is a person who is willing to take such good care of himself that no one else has to. People with centered selves can set their children free, set their spouses free, set their coworkers free, and set themselves free: free to make choices to go, stay, connect, commit, support, and love; free to make all of these choices on a daily basis. This is a position of high self-worth indeed.

A person of high self-worth may appear to be self-centered when actually they are truly a centered self. A low self-worth person needs to use a cover-up for their beliefs about themselves. Manipulated praise is a great paintbrush for self-doubt. It gives a person a means of avoiding the guilt or shame that comes from feeling inadequate.

Joe's Story

When I was five years old, my oldest sister contracted typhoid fever. We lived in a small two-doctor mining town in Colorado. My sister's doctor, Dr. Newland, telephoned

Denver every day to get support and instructions on how to care for her. She was ill for six weeks in the town's little hospital, and he came to our home each night to administer gamma globulin to each of our parents and us three kids. I hated the shots, but I loved the lessons I was learning. He had a magical "doctor bag" that was full of mysterious and powerful tools, instruments, and bandages, and it smelled good, clean and "mediciney." I also learned that this man was special to my mom and dad and, in fact, special to the whole town because he was a doctor. At that point, at age five, I knew I wanted to be a doctor.

A friend of mine illustrates what he calls the all-American career story:

> Little Joey runs into the house and says, "Mommy, Mommy, I want to be a fireman when I grow up!" His mother answers, "Yes, dear, run back out and play." Later he runs into the house and says, "Mommy, Mommy, I want to be a cowboy when I grow up!" and she says, "Yes, Joey, wash your hands for supper." The next day, he runs into the house and shouts, "Mommy, Mommy, I want to be a *doctor* when I grow up!" And the whole Western world comes to a screeching halt. The mother says, "Bert, Grandma, come in here! Did you hear what Joey just said?" The kid is "elected" by the family, and it is difficult to resign the position.

That kid was me. I never took back that statement. I was committed by myself and others. Looking back at that time, I wanted to be a doctor for the accolades it brought me. It is very codependent to strive for a position only for the recognition and self-esteem it brings. That is a perfect example of using something outside of oneself for one's own self-worth. I see now that wanting to be a doctor helped with some of the inadequacy I was feeling in my family. I wanted and needed to be highly thought of in my family.

I continued my quest for accolades throughout grade school, college, and medical school. It was important to me to be president of my junior high classes and my freshman, sophomore, and junior classes. I was not elected president of my high school senior class because I was elected student body president. I continued as president of the Honorary Pre-Med Club at the University of Denver and president of my freshman medical school class at the University of Colorado. All this time, I felt the vulture of self-absorption sitting on my shoulder saying, "You put it over on them . . . you put it over on them." I minimized how I truly felt. There was a lingering feeling of the fear of discovery and punishment. I was engulfed by these feelings (painful feelings, which I later "medicated" with alcohol). These feelings originated in my early life, and the guilt and shame was real—to me. My codependency progressed.

The shame of being inadequate was real to me, but not to the rest of the world, and the rest of the world can be a harsh critic. I know now I must have had much to offer, and I did that. I am grateful for this new knowledge, even now. If I could have been shown my errors in considering myself totally inept and a phony, and if I had had teaching, advice, shared feelings, knowledge, and loving support, my codependency could have been arrested much, much earlier. I lived a doubly confusing life: outer accomplished behavior and inner feelings of self-doubt and inadequacy.

I didn't have loving support in that area because my family was unable to supply it, and later my codependency denial would not let me, you, or anyone know my inaccurate truth that I was "less than." I used the "Leave me alone, I can do it myself!" shield. I would often say, "You shouldn't do that for me"; "What can I do for you?"; and "Of course, I'll be there no matter what happens." I often said to myself, *I'm depressed. I'm a schnook, a nerd; It doesn't matter . . .; I screwed it up again!*

Complications Group Two: Relationship Problems (Disabled Living)

Our bodies, commanded by our brains, can be put on alert in an instant. That alert is the Alarm Reaction that prepares us to fight or flee. Dr. Hans Selye wrote extensively on this concept. The Alarm Reaction is the body's ability to instantaneously get ready to stand ground and fight off a saber-toothed tiger, an opponent in a lawsuit, or the person on the other side of the tennis net. The opposite of that "fight" alarm is the "flight" alarm, which is the body's ability to instantaneously flee in the interest of self-preservation. The heart rate and respiratory rate increase. The amount of oxygen going to the muscles is increased. The muscles tense. All senses become hypervigilant.

As we pass through any given day, we use these defense mechanisms many times over. Although we graciously and outwardly restrain our alarms on most occasions, all of us have been inwardly at war with our social environments from time to time. That environment consists, in part, of family lives, social lives, occupational lives, legal lives, and financial lives.

The codependent lives with environmental wars. The smallest unit is the couple. It is rare to find relationship satisfaction when one is emotionally frozen and behaviorally compulsive. Knowing and responding to a partner is simply not the major focus. Beyond the coupling, family and friends, the job, and the work environment all suffer from a lack of focus and commitment.

When we are at war with ourselves mentally, emotionally, and behaviorally, it is very difficult to be in a close, meaningful relationship with someone else. It is no wonder that in recent years, hundreds of books, articles, and conferences have focused on "intimacy and relationships." Unfortunately, many of these have simplistically suggested that codependency is a "relationship" problem rather than seeing that relationship problems are a *result* and *complication* of codependency.

The notion that codependency is simply being in a relationship with an alcoholic or an addict is an early observation that occurred in the treatment of addictions field. In the early 1970s, it became quite clear that not only were partners and family members affected by being in a relationship with an alcoholic but they were also afflicted with their own disabling illness.

There clearly were problems with:

- dependent relationships
- eating disorders
- excessive caretaking
- nicotine addiction
- workaholism . . .

. . . and many more compulsive behaviors. As these behaviors progressed into complications, the families' own illness of codependency flourished.

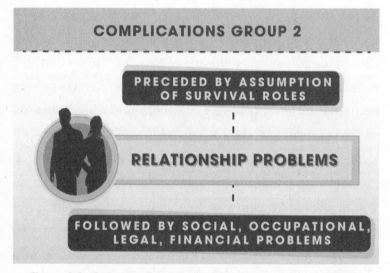

Figure 5.2. Complications Group Two: Relationship Problems

To emphasize only dependent relationships and excessive caretaking as components of this illness is to understand only a small part of codependency. Learning to clearly face the reality of hurting relationships is the first step of recovery. Next comes the behavioral rebuilding of those relationships that one values. Some toxic relationships need to end and others need to be rebuilt. All relationships, whether at work, at home, or out in society, deserve attention in codependency recovery. (For more satisfying relationships, we recommend two books, both by Sharon Wegscheider-Cruse: *Learning to Love Yourself*, which will help you to prepare yourself, and *Coupleship*, which will teach you how to build a partnership.)

An untreated, unattended-to condition in an individual can progress far enough and long enough to result in complications in his or her life. In addition to low self-worth complications, relationship complications arise. These then result in disruptions in the family, such as long absences and emotional distancing on the part of the codependent members. An example of this can be seen in the following story.

Gina got pregnant by accident. She and her boyfriend, Sean, had little doubt that they would get married. They had been together for a couple of years and had already planned some of the wedding; they just hadn't set a date. They were married and had a wonderful baby girl. Sean was busy trying to support them all, and Gina was just as busy trying to be a good mother, housekeeper, and neighbor. Sean kept progressing in his work and Gina started having more babies. He coached Little League and was on a bowling team. She had children who were two, three, four, and five years old. He advanced enough that their oldest could go to college, their second one joined the navy, and their third one earned a scholarship with Gina's help and went to a university.

By the time the youngest was ready to graduate high school, she was already helping Gina in a dress shop downtown. She assured her parents that she liked staying home with them rather than going to college, but shortly thereafter, she married a marine and moved far away. The house was empty, except for the two of them. Things quieted down totally. One morning they woke up, looked at each other, and said, "Who are you?" Their vibrant coupleship had, for the most part, been dormant for twenty-eight years. Their vibrant parenting had taken its place.

The same is true in established friendships. The codependent narrows their interests down to just a few. Work relationships are impacted by lack of motivation and preoccupation. Disruptions can go so far as to unsettle the normal functioning in a person's financial and legal stability.

Complications Group Three: Medical Problems (Disabled Physical Functioning)

If because of low self-worth and shame we do not make changes, we will stay stuck. Stuckness is another word for a subtle death wish. People who are stuck are beginning the dying process. Early in this stuckness we start having medical problems. When we do not reach out to ask for what we need and get ourselves nourished, then our bodies go out of harmony, out of alignment, and out of ease; they become "dis-eased." We make ourselves sick. When we are functioning in harmony, perceiving ourselves as high functioning, we'll be healthier. When we perceive ourselves as low energy, stuck, down, and powerless, we become more susceptible to

illness. The effect of chronic stress on our bodies first pro-
duces many small complaints, ranging from "I'm tired" to
"I ache" and then progresses to organ malfunction, such as
heart irregularity and gastritis to actual organ damage, such
as heart attack or ruptured peptic ulcer.

Stress-related disorders are the most common group of
illnesses the physician encounters. Our bodies have the ability to be constantly on guard for danger. "Stress hormones,"
such as epinephrine, norepinephrine, and cortisol, are
released so that our muscle tone, heart rate, breathing rate,
blood pressure, blood sugar, and other functions are ready to
meet a challenge or flee from danger. Emotional stress, real
or imagined, long-term or sudden, calls our stress hormones
into play, and our bodies respond accordingly.

Organ stress can be likened to an engine that is constantly
running at high RPMs. Every system in the body is going
as fast as it can for as long as it can. Fast, regular heartbeats
(tachycardia), excess acid in our stomach (hyperacidity),
tense muscles (myalgia), rapid breathing (tachypnea), and
increased adrenalin and insulin secretion (hypoglycemia)
are results of a body that is in overdrive. Then our highly
coordinated functions become uncoordinated and we experience malfunctions: irregular heartbeat, uncoordinated
muscles, tremors and shakes, gastritis and cramps, as well as
shortness of breath.

Finally, actual damage results and the body suffers heart failure or heart attacks and/or ruptured ulcers or ulcerative colitis. Lung damage, muscle and nerve damage, or functional fatigue of our glands may also occur. Ruptured vessels or blood clots damage our brain, all of which eliminates us from the race.

Similarly, it is thought that underwork of our bodies might accompany depression and pessimism. Low self-worth can result in a low or nonfunctioning immune system. Our immune system helps us ward off infections and cancer. Thus, when the immune system is dampened or suppressed by negative emotions and attitudes, we become susceptible to diseases.

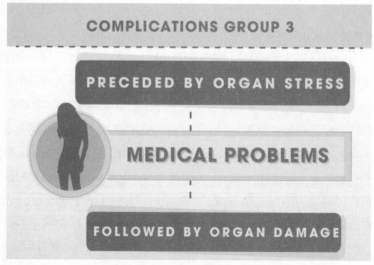

Figure 5.3. Complications Group Three: Medical Problems

HALT

Hungry, Angry, Lonely, and Tired = HALT. This is the acronym that many 12-step groups use to help their members remain aware of what leads to a relapse of their dependency or addiction. Two of these are actually physical, while all four are well-known to cause physical disorders such as acid reflux, high blood pressure, infections and allergies, and accidents. Depression and long-term repression of emotions, and a long-term sense of being less than, can aid and abet, if not result in, diminished immune responses to infection, metabolic disorders, and the formation and growth of malignancies.

Here is an example of physical complications of codependency run rampant. The father in this family was in control of it, and the kids knew where the rules were set down and how to follow them. As a mother, Carol was well-intentioned and wanted only the best for her many children, so she disciplined them according to her own strict upbringing. As a wife, she was showcase pretty and compliant to her husband, and she turned a blind eye to his errors and escapades. She was a gracious partner in his quests for higher office and recognition. She was quiet by nature, but much of her life required she be just the opposite.

Carol began her own career of accomplishments, but it was cut short by abdominal cancer. In those days, no one talked directly about cancer to the patient, to each other, or even to the neighbors; it was only between the doctor, the father, and the kids. Cancer was a whisper word. The family hovered around her during her last months of life, but no one said a single word to her regarding her thirty-four-pound weight loss, the painful gold shots she was getting in her abdomen, or the other "treatments" she was getting for her "stomach condition." Her children gathered together to cook what would be her last Thanksgiving dinner. She was thin, weak, pale, and quiet. They all nervously talked in front of her across the table. No one mentioned her illness in the blessing. Sadly, she later died believing two things: that she did have cancer and that she could trust no one.

Summary

The Life Events that arise from having untreated or incompletely treated codependency result in complications. This is true for any disease. These complications are remarkably similar to the problems a chemically dependent person encounters. To paraphrase, "When we are powerless over our disease, our life becomes unmanageable."

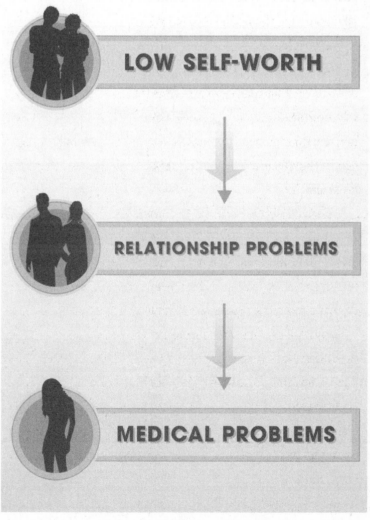

Figure 5.4. Summary of Life Events

CHAPTER 6

Sorting Out Codependency

C harles Whitfield, author of *Co-dependence: Healing the Human Condition*, has often said "Co-dependence is not only the most common addiction, it is the base out of which all our other addictions and compulsions emerge. Underneath nearly every addiction and compulsion lies co-dependence. And what runs them is twofold: a sense of shame that our True Self is somehow defective or inadequate, combined with the innate and healthy drive of our True Self that does not realize and express itself. The addiction, compulsion, or disorder becomes the manifestation of the erroneous notion that something outside ourselves can make us happy and fulfilled."

A touch of codependency occurs in all of us from time to time. Naturally, we react when stressed or affronted. It is when we lose our choices and have to control (compulsion), deny our behavior (denial), and hide our true feelings (repression) that our behaviors begin to interfere with our daily living and the quality of our relationships.

You may be asking yourself, *Where am I in all this? What areas do I need to learn more about? Do I need help? If so, what kind of help is available?* Hopefully this chapter will help you identify with questions that may have arisen as you've read through the book. When approaching the area of codependency and trying to discern if you need to pursue a course of treatment, it is often quite beneficial to have other people involved in retrieving the answers with you. In some cases, in the more difficult areas, it helps to have a group, counselor, or therapist available. Help is available at many levels of intensity. Perhaps it is already obvious to you that recovery from codependency is not a solo job. The levels of help, the types of help, and the efforts needed in treatment vary with each of us. One approach to sorting it out is to use Brain

Events and Life Events as they apply to you. Give these events a hard, honest look.

Sorting Out Brain Events

Denial

We need to practice rigorous, if not tortuous, self-honesty to admit to ourselves and others that we have been in denial. Self-assessment tests, such as those included in Chapter 9, will help you determine where you're at on the spectrum of codependency (you can also find self-assessment tests online at www.coda.org). It is not enjoyable to look at ourselves and see what we have been covering up or how we have rationalized the choices we've made in order to avoid pain or responsibility. Many times we cannot admit responsibility for an action because we really believe it is untrue. Here the use of others is particularly helpful. Speaking frankly and openly to a friend, pastor, or 12-step sponsor can be very helpful if we are ready to hear whatever they have to say.

Denial can be so subtle that it evens fools others around us, which is why we use it. Find someone who cares enough and is strong enough to "say it as they see it"—and who is capable enough and patient enough to carry on a "denial debate" with you. As Proverbs 27:6 says, "Faithful are the wounds of a friend." While it may hurt us to hear the truth, it is for our ultimate good. If we have a friend who can tell us the truth with love, that person is a blessing indeed.

Sometimes the breakthrough of denial is subtle and extends over a period of time. Therapeutic and 12-step support groups are a great help. So often in a group, one hears, "That woman was telling my story!" and the barriers come down. When we recognize denial and minimizing in others' lives, it often becomes more apparent in our own.

The most intense attack on denial can come in the form of a formal intervention. This is popularly used for alcoholics and addicts, though it works as well for other forms of codependency that have run rampant in a loved one. A person's family, friends, and possibly employer may hire a professional interventionist to train them as a team and lead a family meeting where each member of the intervention team presents specific data regarding the thinking and behavior they see in the codependent, what their feelings are about it, how it has affected them, and what the agreed-upon consequences will be if the behavior continues.

In an intervention, someone may say something similar to this at the family meeting: "Mom, you know why we are here. We love you, but we are extremely upset with the way you have been treating Dad and us. Last week, you were screaming the day before, the day of, and the day after our family reunion. You seem to do that more and more lately if we don't bow to your way of doing things. It is embarrassing, especially in front of others. I am angry and I was sad and shocked when you slapped Billy's hand with a ladle at the table. I want to be around you, but if you can't follow a plan we are recommending, I will not be able to be around you. It hurts too much. Dad and the kids will speak for themselves."

What often happens when denial is broken is that the individual looks as though an impenetrable black mask has been lifted from their eyes. They look around, wide-eyed, as if to say, "I didn't know it was so bad!" And they're often telling the truth.

Emotional Repression: The Abscess

How can we do emotional surgery on ourselves? We don't need to and we don't have to. In fact, we probably shouldn't. One of the most liberating and bonding things a person can engage in is to share feelings with another. The sharing of stuffed feelings in an emotional abscess can be even more bonding. Sharing difficult emotions can bring up all kinds of feelings, to say the least, and sometimes this is very painful.

Many of us have been told to "Watch your temper," "Go to your room until you can quit crying," and that "Men are strong!" Good! But can men be strong and still be emotional?

Women like a strong man, and even more so when he is emotionally available, sensitive, and empathetic. Many men have been taught to relinquish these attributes in order to appear strong. Women are more outwardly emotional, sensitive, and delicate. They have a secret: they don't usually relinquish their incredible strength; they just conceal it in order to appear feminine.

Buried emotions silently work away at our sense of well-being, our blood pressure, our immune system, and our physical health in many ways. Once an emotional abscess is opened, positive changes start occurring quite quickly. Hope comes flying out of the wound, and determination and a commitment to change follow close behind. How is this emotional surgery performed? The basis of it is the calling up of associated events with the feelings. Often the memories that have lain dormant in the abscess serve as a hook that gives rise to the negative and fearful emotions that lie within. Because revealing these negative and fearful emotions can be quite traumatic, this type of treatment is best done with the help of a therapist.

Emotional abscesses can begin early in a person's life and often grow larger throughout the years. Rickie's story is a good example of this. Rickie and James were friends from the fourth grade. They were from a small town, which allowed for much crossover in activities and interests. They were in the school band together, attended the same church youth group, and went to church camp together every summer. They had parents in the same card club.

They mainly differed in that Rickie was two years younger than James and came from a family of seven, while James was an only child and got his own way in most things. James's toys far outshined Rickie's, but he was generous with them. By the time they were in high school, the two-year difference in age made quite a difference in behavior. Rickie tried to do his best to please James, who called the shots for Rickie and many other boys in town.

When they got to college, James was living in his own apartment off campus. Rickie and one of his brothers were living in their grandma's basement bedroom near the university. The envy and sadness Rickie felt were well hidden from everyone. The jealousy and anger at having to "follow James's orders" never showed, but when James seduced Rickie's high school sweetheart in his private apartment after a college dance, that was it. Rickie managed his feelings by avoiding James and his former sweetheart from that time on.

Years later, Rickie was in dire straits, even though he had a successful career. His wife of twenty years had an affair, he attempted suicide, and his emotional abscess had grown to enormous proportions as he had stuffed his emotions time and again for many years. In his search for relief, he found himself in a therapy group that used experiential techniques to open emotional abscesses.

He was guided through role playing, where he could face, feel, and reenact emotional events that had been painful to him. He expressed his emotions loudly and with authority. He angrily tore up magazines while expressing his feelings toward his ex-wife. He used a bat on a pillow to discharge the anger he felt toward James, screaming and swearing and feeling the pent-up anger that had lain unexpressed for years and years. Surprisingly, he wasn't angry about his college sweetheart. Rather, it was the anger he had stuffed during those nights at church camp in the bunkhouse when James had forced Rickie to masturbate him and then laughed when he ejaculated all over him. Exposure and expression of the many emotional toxins built up throughout the years gave Rickie untold relief and freedom. He was no longer suicidal, and the all-too-familiar pit in his stomach faded away.

The purpose of calling up emotions is so they can be identified and discharged. The goal is to cancel their effects on us. We cannot put a salve or any other medication on them and expect a permanent cure; if they remain hidden, they will eventually return or just propagate more of the same. We need to discharge them from the depths of the abscess once and for all. Anger needs to be released, grief needs to be expressed, forgiveness needs to be experienced, acceptance needs to be learned and felt, and so on. Then the abscess can heal from the inside out. Again, this type of therapy is most often done with a professional.

Ongoing healing and the prevention of a future abscess are up to each of us. We must remain watchful for those times when we withhold expressing our emotions or when we are not able to even honestly describe them after an event. It can be healing and bonding to arrange an appointment, even long after an affront you may have suffered, to express your latent feelings to the perpetrator. Describing our feelings passes the information on to the other person and helps us to not just act on the basis of our emotions about the event. Taking an inventory at bedtime and noting the residual emotional energy that remains is half the battle. Sometimes jotting down the emotion on a notepad on the bedside table and waiting until morning to deal with it will allow for a more sound sleep. Just as Scarlett O'Hara said in *Gone with the Wind*, "Tomorrow is another day!" You can deal with it the next morning (only minus Scarlett's constant state of denial).

Emotions can be neutralized quite often by writing them into a personal journal each morning or by meditating on them until they are gone. Often we can learn from an emotion that just seems to keep hanging around. When we actually analyze, share, or write down a fear or a feeling of sadness or anger, we may reveal its true origin and find a direction for resolution.

Compulsion

When a person cannot consistently refrain from a certain behavior, and cannot refrain from it even when it has adverse consequences attached to it, we say he or she has a compulsion to control another, to please everyone, and so on. Doing such things results in a false sense of self-worth and some temporary rewards in the form of relief or excitement. These are Brain Events from the reward/pleasure center in the brain. As we explored in Chapter 1, compulsive pathways are set up in the brain, and it is very hard to modify them. We move from being a Choicemaker to being powerless. When we face our compulsive behaviors and decide to change them, we need every strategy we can find.

Recent cultural changes have occurred because of technology. Instant availability and connection has impacted and permeated most relationships. The pressure and stress of feeling that we must respond to every phone call, text message, or e-mail has produced a subtle and intense feeling of always being "on" and available. There are many reasons why this is so. Some people are afraid they will miss out on something if they don't stay connected. Others place a value on themselves because they are so involved. This is not to underestimate the wonderful function of technology, including making life so much easier by keeping track of children and parents, being available during emergencies, and being a convenient way to send quick messages that solve many problems. The list of modern technology's plus side could go on and on.

What we are referring to here is the constant text messaging, talking, and e-mailing that is not necessary at all times, such as when standing in checkout lines in grocery stores, discount stores, and security lines at airports. (Imagine actually being forced to listen to an argument between an adult daughter and her mother while waiting to go through an airport security line. The daughter said to her mother, "Just a minute; I am putting you through the scanner and I will pick you up on the other side," which she did).

No one really wants to listen to another's conversation in a restaurant, theater, elevator, waiting line, or shopping area. It is frightening to make a left turn in a crowded double lane while the driver next to you is turning with one hand while having an animated conversation on his cell phone.

Quite often, you see only the bowed heads of those people who are texting in a group. It is difficult to believe you are being heard and understood. Conversational skills classes are now including a section on preoccupation with technology.

These classes teach people how to talk in a social group, such as what you say, how you look into someone's eyes as you speak, and how you register how you are being received.

Many younger people have missed out on the art of making conversation today. They have grown up with e-mail and texting that is readily available. Social skills are underdeveloped in this group, yet they will need these skills at many points in their lives. They do not need nor should they suffer from a total fixation on their "devices." This kind of dependency erodes a person's identity, self-worth, and true connection with others. They are tethered by an electronic connection rather than connected to people directly.

An illustration of how technology can become a compulsion is clearly seen in Mark's life. Mark has his phone on during all his waking hours. He sends and receives texts and calls during all his available time. For him, even e-mail is becoming too slow. His communications are primarily texting or spending time on Facebook or Twitter.

Jan is trying to establish a relationship with Mark. She is frustrated and definitely feels second to his "tethered" self. He checks his e-mail first thing every morning. He sneaks out of the bedroom hoping she'll sleep in so he can read texts, newsletters, and e-mail. He is on the Internet late into the evening and often gets distracted "looking up things." Hours go by before he notices.

Jan feels she is not connected to Mark in the same way he is connected to his equipment. She wants to be engaged and is thinking she needs to leave the relationship and find a person with whom she can engage and connect. She wants someone who can use technology rather than let it use him. Mark's need to be tethered to his world through electronics has become very compulsive and is impacting his primary relationship.

Compulsive behavior is often so subconscious that we hardly realize we are indulging in it. Like so many other aspects of our lives, we are unaware of the here and now for extended periods of time. We cannot refrain or modify a compulsive behavior if we are unaware of it. We need to keep our guard up for it, or our brains will sneak it in on us. We need to be mindful. We need to be vigilant during our waking hours and interrupt any thoughts and behaviors that have caused us difficulty in the past.

We need to stay in the here and now. If we are preoccupied with an event from the past, or we are preoccupied with concerns for some future happening, then we have our eyes off the present and what the brain is up to. The past is past and the future isn't here yet; it doesn't pay to dwell on it over and over (though this does not mean that the past can't be rectified nor the future prepared for). Just knowing this simple truth helps us to remain mindful. Much has been written on the subject of mindfulness that is helpful for recovering from compulsive codependency (for example, see Jon Kabat-Zinn, some of whose book titles are included in the Bibliography at the end of the book).

> **Energy flows where attention goes.**
> —Hawaiian saying

What Is Needed Is to "Train Your Brain"

Compulsions are one area of brain function that reveals its true nature. As shown in Chapter 1, this marvelous, amazing, mysterious organ acts like a spoiled little child from time to time. It says, "I want what I want when I want it, and I want it right now!" Just like that spoiled child, our brains occasionally need discipline and training. When a mindful person catches herself in big-time codependent behavior or thoughts, she needs to stop and record that fact. How can she record it? One way is by using a "mantra count." As mentioned in Chapter 1, a mantra is a Hindu or Buddhist saying or prayer that is repeated over and over as an aid in concentration or focus. It becomes ingrained in the person's head and can actually change his or her behavior. Keep these events general and simple. Say to yourself, *I don't do that anymore,* or write on a pad or journal, "I don't do that anymore," or tell a friend, "I don't do that anymore."

Call a friend to help you with mindfulness and your mantra count. Ask him or her to help you see the full extent of your behavior. Telling a therapy or 12-step group also works well, as many of them have "been there, done that." The group will bounce back their experiences and reinforce your brain so that recovery pathways light up and codependency pathways dim down. Your brain can learn and relearn. Read about codependency; accept your codependency and your brain will learn. It becomes clear that just as in chemical dependency, in codependency we need help. We need others —maybe all types of others—to help us. We need "cheering squads."

> It is difficult to recover from
> codependency in secret.

Sorting Out Life Events

Self-Worth

Guilt and shame and the role they play in our sense of self have been described in Chapter 5. Tina's story is a good example of how guilt and shame operate in our lives. Tina didn't know it, but she had a tough spot in the family. Her oldest sister could do no wrong, and her dad even counted on her sister to help out with the family business. Tina noticed that her sister and her mother had a lot of secrets between them, and both of them became irritated when Tina would ask about them.

Tina's older brother was always in trouble, and her younger brother was always shoving his way in, being silly, and getting attention. She felt better in her room by herself. She had hand-me-down clothes, which she hated, and books, which she loved. It was nice when she would receive an occasional compliment about how well behaved she was compared to her brothers.

She was afraid to go to school and was always preoccupied and kept a watch out for the group of girls that would insult, tease, and actually push her around. She talked her mom into finally writing an excuse for her to skip gym class, where the girls were at their worst. She took the shortest route possible to get home, skipping any after-school socializing. She truly believed she was flawed and less than and probably deserved the bullying. She was depressed. She wondered if the rod in the closet and one of her belts could stop it all, or if a handful of her mom's pills would give her permanent relief: the ultimate act of self-loathing. In truth, she didn't want to be dead; she just didn't want to live the life she had been living.

Society sends us messages every day. Unless our families correct these messages and unless our schools, government, and institutions send out person-centered messages, they go uncorrected and we believe them. If we, our families, and others do not correct these messages and replace them with messages of high self-worth, it becomes difficult to refute them. We may attempt to refute them with our own error messages to give us a feeling of (false) self-worth: "I am a member of . . ."; "I am a new car owner"; "I am always willing to . . ."; "I am a good golfer"; "I am the best dresser"; "I am in charge"; "I am right about that"; "I am a great employee"; "Look at me; see what I do?"

> If what you do is who you are . . .
> and you don't . . . you ain't!
> —A woodcarver

We are each unique on this earth; there is not another exactly like us. Even identical twins are not totally the same in chromosomes, enzymes, perceptions, experiences, and responses. We are an amazing array of living cells that house a soul. We are precious human beings because we exist. We are blessed to be alive and our lives are a blessing to others.

Finding Personal Self-Worth

The search for our self-worth is an active one and requires both passive observation and active participation. We need to unlearn any misconceptions we have, identify any erroneous feelings and behaviors, and regain any self-confidence in ourselves that may have gone unused for too long.

All this is based on the idea that we had self-worth at one time and then it was lost. That is true. When we were babies, we couldn't differentiate between ourselves and the outside world or another person. Then, at a few months of age, we learned some remarkable things. We had hands and arms that could reach and hold things. We were separate and different than those faces that looked down into our crib and made funny faces and sounds. We didn't know why, but it was much more pleasurable to be held than to lie alone in the crib. There was no thought that we were anything less than just right, perfect, and special. How was it lost, this self-worth of ours? More important, how do we get it back and not mistake those things that give us pseudo-self-worth as the real thing?

Tina's father was successful. He was successful for many years at providing for his family and successful in being a long-term, controlled alcoholic. The disease of alcoholism won out and he ended up in an addiction treatment center that insisted each member of the family attend their own therapy programs. They were not there just to learn what happened in their family of origin, but more important, they were there to discover their needs and how to meet them.

Thinking Positive

Positive affirmations replace negative affirmations. Take a negative message you have received and reverse it. Tina and her father came up with this:

> *Example:* "Go to your room and stay there until you get control of your emotions!"
>
> *Reversed:* "Your feelings are important; let's figure this out."

> Our emotions are a God-given
> gift to us. They help protect us in times of
> threat; they help to describe us in times
> of connecting with others; they affirm us in
> times of reflection; they give us insight
> in times of deliberation.

Positive Affirmations Spontaneously Given

Tina and her group were each given a sheet of computer labels. They were then instructed to write a positive affirmation for her and present it to her as a badge to wear. This was done for each member of the group. They all ended up looking as though they were wearing a vest of medals. They were surprised at the opinions of the others and the warm feelings this gave them. We live in a world of many people. Naturally, the opinions of others are important to us. This is fine, as long as the search for a good opinion does not drive us into compulsively seeking it.

Setting Boundaries

Tina was able to sit in front of the group with each member of her family. She was able to tell her dad she was afraid he would die while driving home drunk. She was able to tell her sister she felt left out of the loop of "girl talk" at their house. She was able to tell her mother she needed new things to wear once in a while. She was able to ask her younger brother to leave her things alone and not jump on her bed all the time. She asked her older brother to watch out for her at school and to be more aware of his terrific temper because it scared her. She told them all she loved them. She felt strong and relieved when they heard her.

Some of the most difficult decisions we have to make each day are those dealing with boundaries. What are we willing to do or not do? How far will we go in answer to another's wishes? What is harmless and what are harmful allowances and permissions? We teach others how to treat us. If we don't, they decide how they will treat us—and continue to treat us—if we do not teach them differently.

Memories Can Be Our Friends

Tina forgot that at one time she was the family musician. When her father reminded her with a computer label, and stated that he had told his employees about her top piano recital last year, she felt the warm glow of praise. But her label didn't just describe one event; it said "A Natural Musician." She then remembered the difficult time she had with geometry, but she worked on it until she liked it—and then she aced the course. The group asked her to recall other accomplishments she might have forgotten and to take them in as useful, good, and worth remembering. Upon returning home, she found herself looking in the mirror each morning and winking.

Codependency often insists on perfection. Anything less than perfect is imperfect. Codependents describe accomplishments as "not good enough" or "not as good as," therefore, they cannot see the usefulness of their accomplishments, which become useless in their minds and are quickly discounted and forgotten. Thus, the codependent, through association, is one titch less useful also. Tina retained some of the friendships she made at the treatment program, joined an Adult Children of Alcoholics (ACoA) group, and grew up to become a wife, mother, and teacher of music theory at a local college.

Spirituality

Within our self-worth is our spirituality. Spirituality requires that we believe our bodies, brains, and lives are precious. The most precious part of us is our souls. In fact, we are not our bodies. We are given our bodies as marvelous, beautifully designed Land Rovers for moving us around this planet. We are inside there somewhere looking out, and God is driving. More and more often we hear this great self-worth phrase: "I am me! Hooray!"

Relationships

The most valued relationship we can have is our primary relationship. What a task! To balance what one's needs are against what one is willing to give is the greatest balancing act we encounter in life. It is not a primary or singular event because we change as we proceed through life. Therefore, our personal checks and balances must be continuously reviewed, acknowledged, and modified. So must those of our partners. Marriage vows and partnership agreements may change a bit each day. They are not just singular events to state what you need and will contribute to the relationship; they need to be implied, if not actually stated, each day. The behavior and the willingness of each partner usually do the implying. It is a delicate and intricate dance to maintain equal balance in a "coupleship," but it is worth every effort. To have a true soul mate is one of the basic blessings of life.

> Balancing your life between work, play, spirituality, exercise, and relationships helps you grow and feel joy.
>
> —Doreen Virtue

Because our primary relationship is so delicate, it is susceptible to damage from even the slightest attack of codependency in either partner. For example, if either person has a great need to control, has a point of focus greater than the coupleship, is of low self-worth, is more fixed on people and events outside the coupleship, or has an addiction of any type, then codependency has invaded and needs to be repulsed if the coupleship is to survive, as shown in the following story about Mark and Megan.

Mark and Megan were considered a perfect couple. He was athletic and a leader, and she was pretty, talented, and popular. They had college degrees, came from supportive families, and attended the same church. It surprised no one when they got married after Mark had landed a great job. Eight years and three children later, they were painfully considering divorce. Family, friends, and clergy counseling could not help them restore what they once had. They were at an impasse and had run out of patience trying to "figure it out." It was not a conflict about the divorce settlement—they hadn't gotten that far yet—nor did they actually want to. They were just muddling, complaining, and enduring. They agreed to attend a couples program as a last-ditch effort, and it was through this avenue that they learned that the battle for independence of the coupleship has to be joined on three fronts: excess emotional baggage, invaders, and minefields.

- **Excess Emotional Baggage.** We each bring excess emotional baggage to a coupleship. It comes in the form of continuing dependence and preoccupation on the family of origin, a previous relationship, or special friends. Unrelenting memories and dependency on a former job or activity or group can be excess baggage. (Mark and Megan agreed to negotiate open-mindedly with others, together and with each other.)

- **Invaders.** Invaders of a coupleship include children, jobs/careers, overdependence on close friends, or too much dependency and focus on an activity or an institution. (Mark and Megan agreed to continue to teach the kids that they are valued members of their family, but that their coupleship was separate and required respect. They agreed to negotiate with open minds regarding other invaders.)

- **Minefields.** There are minefields in the future (such as financial worries, unexpected illnesses, etc.). These are problems that can tip a coupleship by their sudden appearance and perplexing management. (Mark and Megan agreed that some mines in the minefield are best avoided on the advice of one or the other of them, and others are avoided best by the advice of both of them.)

A coupleship is a distinct entity. Mark and Megan stood on three chairs. Megan had one foot on her "personal chair" and one foot on the "couples chair"; Mark had one foot on his "personal chair" and one foot also on the "couples chair." They hugged and became aware that they were a formidable triangular fortress. They were shown that they could manage any excess baggage and ward off invaders, and from their high position, they had early warning of oncoming minefields. They both had invested a part of themselves in the coupleship without losing their personal identities, as demonstrated by their personal chairs. They could be together and yet "Let the winds of heaven dance between them!" (Kahlil Gibran, *The Prophet*).

They experienced critiqued negotiations as they sat on chairs in the center of the group circle, eye to eye, hand to hand, and knees to knees. The group members and therapists were able to comment as Mark and Megan found insight and clarity.

- They saw negotiations in action as they observed other couples in the group participating.

- They were given a chance to remember an old happy memory: a second chance to dress for, attend, and enjoy a prom night.

- They showed a renewed interest in humor and play.

- They were given plans of action for each of them personally and for the coupleship.

- They gratefully expressed hope, motivation, and a commitment to do their very best to find the best in their relationship.

Other Relationships

Codependency can cause disruptions in our relationships at work, with friends, and in our financial lives. The manner in which we handle our position with coworkers, employers, and employees will determine how successful we will be. Excessive attention and inattention, and intrusion and avoidance, are equally disruptive. There is a productive and happy medium. Excessive attention or inattention to our financial and investment lives can also cripple us and deprive us of financial independence. These and other relationships, along with a sense of high self-worth, provide much of the basis for a happy and meaningful life. We must guard against the complications of codependency that threaten to take those relationships and that meaningful life from us.

Final Complication: Medical Problems

A vast amount of literature exists on the subject of our minds and its influence on our bodies. The impact of codependency can be great. A description of the mechanism by which we become ill through our thoughts, behaviors, and beliefs is simply stated on pages 88–93. Information on the effects of our emotions on our immune systems has expanded and taken an important place in the development of malignant disease and our susceptibility to autoimmune diseases (see, for example, Norman Cousins, *Anatomy of an Illness*). If this is true, then we must assume that recovering from codependency and major codependent behaviors will enable and even accelerate our recovery from physical diseases.

Summary

Brain Events of Codependency
Denial
Repression of Feelings
Compulsions
These can be called the Symptoms.

Life Events of Codependency
Low Self-Worth
Relationship Problems
Medical Problems
These can be called the Complications.

> We must let go of the life
> we have planned in order to find
> the life that is waiting for us.
>
> —Joseph Campbell

CHAPTER 7

Treatment and Recovery

Effective Treatment

The miracle of recovery is there for those who choose to make new choices and decisions. The good news is that codependency is treatable. But what is the best treatment?

1. Effective treatment confronts self-delusion with new information. With learning comes understanding

and insight, and from that comes a reality-based commitment to heal.

2. Effective treatment creates a safe atmosphere where feelings can surface and be expressed and discharged so healing can take place. We can't heal what we can't feel.

3. Effective treatment provides an atmosphere where it is safe and possible to recognize, detox, and detach from compulsive medicating behaviors. We can't feel what is medicated.

The Codependent and Recovery

The codependent does best with a two-part recovery program. One part is involvement in a 12-step group and the other part is a relationship with a codependency therapist or a professionally led group.

> The miracle of recovery is there for those who choose to make new choices and decisions.

So often we see codependents who are attending three or four different kinds of 12-step programs, and perhaps a leaderless Adult Children of Alcoholics group, but who are not getting any professional therapy. People in this kind of situation are often confused, angry, and overwhelmed. Even though they go to many meetings, they still do not feel focused or in recovery. As people uncover more and more memories and begin to feel more, their life situations become more complex. It is important for these people to get professional care. They need help to make the necessary decisions, to receive guidance while uncovering feelings, and to have input and a reality check by someone qualified to give it.

> The major compulsion that one exhibits can be the doorway to a program of recovery. One can work through any compulsion with the 12 steps and does not need to go to separate groups for each issue.

It is not necessary to go to many different types of 12-step programs. The focus of 12-step work is to use the steps to work through solutions rather than rehashing and reliving the problems. These 12-step groups work well whether one is concerned with compulsive eating, compulsive gambling, compulsive acting out sexually, or any of the other addictions. The major compulsion that one exhibits can be the doorway to a program of recovery.

One can work through any compulsion with the 12 steps and does not need to go to separate groups for each issue. One or two groups should suffice, for instance, Alcoholics Anonymous (AA) and Overeaters Anonymous (OA), Narcotics Anonymous (NA) and Adult Children of Alcoholics (ACoA), and so on. Therefore, we recommend that people pick one or two 12-step programs to attend that fit with the major compulsion they are struggling with. They should then reserve time and energy to invest in a therapeutic process that is intense and behavior-change oriented.

When one picks a therapist to work with in codependency recovery, it's important to choose someone who thoroughly understands the disease concept of codependency. If that person has come from a painful family of his own, it is crucial that he has already received treatment and is healing in his own treatment process.

Therapy can come in many forms. It can be an outpatient program, or it can be a short, intense program, lasting from eight to ten days. It is important that the program be designed and facilitated by people who are specifically trained in codependency work. Formal continuous therapy can and does come to an end.

> Formal continuous therapy can
> and does come to an end.

Involvement in a 12-step program can be a much longer commitment. A good treatment program is like emotional surgery: it is a good place to do a lot of work all at once. Emotional surgery is then followed by a period of expert care and is accompanied by long-term healing, which takes place in 12-step support groups. Prevention of relapse is also provided by 12-step groups.

Think of recovery as a large, beautiful mansion, as in Figure 7.1, with all kinds of doors and rooms for exploration. Here we can find new styles and new horizons. The mansion is there for anyone who wants to walk through a door. One can come in through the door of alcoholism, the door of sexual compulsion, the door of eating disorders, or the door of workaholism. Each one of these doors is an entry point that you can recognize for yourself. Once you walk through the door, the differences are diminished and the similarities emphasized.

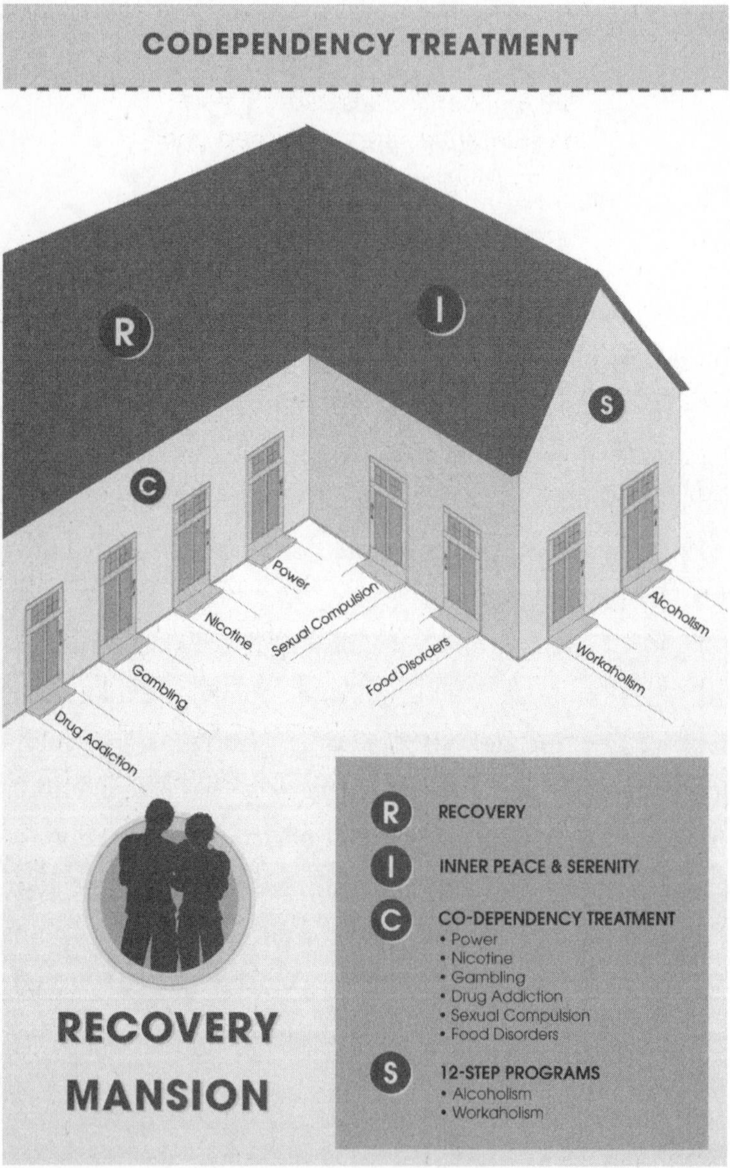

Figure 7.1. Recovery Mansion

Once you walk through the door,
the differences are diminished and
the similarities emphasized.

The disease of codependency can be seen as a personal struggle with a variety of compulsive diseases. People walking through the door have lived in a condition of denial, distorted feelings, and compulsive behaviors, and as a result they have developed low self-worth, deep shame, inadequacy, and anger. All people inside the mansion are exploring and looking for the same recovery route. They are searching for a healing of self. Once through the door, we are all much more alike than different; our differences can now fade and together we can focus on recovery in a supportive, simple, and clear manner.

Recovery Requirements

The Disease Results in ...	Recovery and Healing Require That We ...
Denial/Self-delusion	admit our lives are unmanageable and we need help.
Emotional repression	stop medicating feelings with substances and behaviors and allow ourselves to reconnect with feelings in our lives.
Compulsive behavior	become abstinent from toxic substances and moderate compulsive behaviors.
Chronic low self-worth	take the risks and make the changes to care for oneself.
Relationship problems	change behaviors to rebuild valued relationships and end or change toxic ones.
Medical problems	seek appropriate medical help.

Most compulsive behaviors are extreme exaggerations of natural and normal behavior (work, eating, spending, sexuality, etc.) and require moderation for recovery. Use of mood-altering substances, such as drugs or alcohol, requires abstinence for full recovery. (For a complete manual on how to treat codependency on an outpatient and/or inpatient basis, see *Experiential Therapy for Co-dependency* by the Cruses and George Bougher.)

CHAPTER 8

Recovering Alcoholics and Addicts

The concept of codependency began as a description of the disordered manner in which family members of alcoholics reacted to the drinker, and treatment programs did more to alienate family members than help them create healthy relationships: chemically dependent versus the codependent; the AA member versus the Al-Anon/Alateen member; the "sick one" (the alcoholic) versus the "struggling to keep it together ones" (the nonalcoholic family members).

The polarity that resulted was great enough in programming and practices that the alcoholic almost became a family non-member.

Therapists and counselors reinforced these mistaken attitudes with statements such as:

"Do you agree with the alcoholic or the family members?"

"Should the alcoholics attend this family orientation?"

"I prefer to treat the alcoholic and not the family member."

Such actions, concepts, and statements tend to exclude two important factors: (1) the alcoholic/addict is a family member, and (2) the alcoholic/addict is a codependent. *Scratch the paint off a chemical dependent and you will find a full-blown codependent.* Codependency accompanies, and usually precedes, chemical dependency. It precipitates but does not cause chemical dependency.

Again, it is important to understand that codependency does not cause chemical dependency, other than as a stimulus for the use of certain substance medicators. Genetic programming is probably the major reason that the use of mood-altering drugs provides the degree and type of reinforcement that leads to dependency on chemicals. Ten percent of adults have this programming. An additional 10 percent use these chemicals in a medicating and abusive manner.

Symptom Reemergence

When the substance medicators such as alcohol and nicotine are removed and an individual becomes abstinent, the previously medicated codependency symptoms fully emerge once again. (This is frequently seen in psychiatry when, for example, a patient becomes depressed again after a successful antidepressant is withdrawn.)

Bill W.'s Recovery

Bill Wilson (1895–1971), cofounder of Alcoholics Anonymous and author of the book *12 Steps and 12 Traditions*, suffered greatly from depression and migraines. These even drove him back to certain chemicals in order to gain some degree of relief. He tried megadoses of vitamin E, which caused flushing. He attempted to make a case for its use as an antidepressant for recovering alcoholics. His colleagues discouraged his efforts. He briefly tried LSD and other drugs, being unaware at that time of the problems of cross addiction. Thankfully, he did not relapse into active alcoholism.

The early (1935–45) and middle (1945–55) years of AA were tumultuous and chaotic. It took a strong hand and a definite sense of purpose to be the central figure in the movement. Bill's prior alcoholism took its toll on his family, career, and physical health. He discovered the source of his pathological compulsions, controlling of others, depression, and migraines when he discovered his own codependency.

His dependency on "people, events, and things" outside himself for his self-worth drove him into a painful sobriety. Once he realized this and was able to release his dependencies, he became capable of one-way giving. He then became the recipient of the tranquillity he had assumed would come with abstinence. He finally attained emotional sobriety as well. He began his recovery from the disorder of codependency without even knowing its name. Here is his story.

> There is no need to suffer through a painful sobriety.

LOVE

THE NEXT FRONTIER
Emotional Sobriety

by Bill W.[1]

I think that many oldsters who have put our AA "booze cure" to severe but successful tests still find they often lack emotional sobriety. Perhaps they will be the spearhead for the next major development in AA—the development of much more real maturity and balance (which is to say, humility) in our relations with ourselves, with our fellows and with God.

Those adolescent urges that so many of us have for top approval, perfect security and perfect romance—urges quite appropriate to age 17—prove to be an impossible way of life when we are at age 47 or 57.

Since AA began, I've taken immense wallops in all these areas because of my failure to grow up, emotionally and spiritually. My God, how painful it is to keep demanding the impossible and how very painful to discover finally that all along we have had the cart before the horse! Then comes the final agony of seeing how awfully wrong we have been, but still finding ourselves unable to get off the emotional merry-go-round.

---

[1] Copyright 1958 by the AA *Grapevine*, Inc. Reprinted by permission.

How to translate a right mental conviction into a right emotional result and so into easy, happy and good living—well, that's not only the neurotic's problem, it's the problem of life itself for all of us who have got to the point of real willingness to hew to right principles in all our affairs.

Even then, as we hew away, peace and joy will still elude us. That's the place so many of us AA oldsters have come to. And it's a hell of a spot, literally. How shall our unconscious—from which so many of our fears, compulsions and phony aspirations still stream—be brought into line with what we actually believe, know and want? How to convince our dumb, raging and hidden "Mr. Hyde" becomes our main task.

I've recently come to believe that this can be achieved. I believe so because I begin to see many benighted ones—folks like you and me—commencing to get results. Last autumn [several years back—ed.] depression, having no really rational cause at all, almost took me to the cleaners. I began to get scared that I was in for another long chronic spell. Considering the grief I've had with depressions, it wasn't a bright prospect.

I kept asking myself, "Why can't the 12 Steps work to release depression?" By the hour, I stared at the St. Francis Prayer . . . "It's better to comfort than to be comforted." Here was the formula all right. But why didn't it work?

Suddenly I realized what the matter was. My basic flaw had always been dependence—almost absolute dependence—on people or circumstances to supply me with prestige, security and the like. Failing to get these things according to my perfectionist dreams and specifications, I had fought for them. And when defeat came, so did my depression.

There wasn't a chance of making the outgoing love of St. Francis a workable and joyous way of life until these fatal and almost absolute dependencies were cut away.

Because I had over the years undergone a little spiritual development, the absolute quality of these frightful dependencies had never before been so starkly revealed. Reinforced by what Grace I could secure in prayer, I found I had to exert every ounce of will and action to cut off these faulty emotional dependencies upon people, upon AA, indeed, upon any set of circumstances whatsoever.

Then only could I be free to love as St. Francis had. Emotional and instinctual satisfactions, I saw, were really the extra dividends of having love, offering love, and expressing a love appropriate to each relationship of life.

Plainly, I could not avail myself of God's love until I was able to offer it back to Him by loving others as He would have me. And I couldn't possibly do that so long as I was victimized by false dependencies.

For my dependency meant demand—a demand for the possession and control of the people and the conditions surrounding me.

While those words "absolute dependency" may look like a gimmick, they were the ones that helped to trigger my release into my present degree of stability and quietness of mind, qualities which I am now trying to consolidate by offering love to others regardless of the return to me.

This seems to be the primary healing circuit: an outgoing love of God's creation and His people, by means of which we avail ourselves of His love for us. It is most clear that the real current can't flow until our paralyzing dependencies are broken and broken at depth. Only then can we possibly have a glimmer of what adult love really is.

Spiritual calculus, you say? Not a bit of it. Watch any AA of six months working with a new Twelfth Step case. If the case says, "To the devil with you," the Twelfth Stepper only smiles and turns to another case. He doesn't feel frustrated or rejected. If his next case responds and in turn starts to give love and attention to other alcoholics, yet gives none back to him, the sponsor is happy about it anyway. He still doesn't feel rejected; instead he rejoices that his onetime prospect is sober and happy. And if his next case turns out in later time to be his best friend (or romance), then the sponsor is most joyful. But he well knows that his happiness is a byproduct—the extra dividend of giving without any demand for a return.

The really stabilizing thing for him was having and offering love to that strange drunk on his doorstep. That was St. Francis at work, powerful and practical, minus dependency and minus demand.

In the first six months of my own sobriety, I worked hard with many alcoholics. Not a one responded. Yet this work kept me sober. It wasn't a question of those alcoholics giving me anything. My stability came out of trying to give, not out of demanding that I receive.

Thus I think it can work out with emotional sobriety. If we examine every disturbance we have, great or small, we will find at the root of it some unhealthy dependency and its consequent unhealthy demand. Let us, with God's help, continually surrender these hobbling demands. Then we can be set free to live and love; we may then be able to Twelfth Step ourselves and others into emotional sobriety.

Of course, I haven't offered you a really new idea—only a gimmick that has started to unhook several of my own "hexes" at depth. Nowadays my brain no longer races compulsively in either elation, grandiosity or depression. I have been given a quiet place in bright sunshine.

CHAPTER 9

Self-Assessment

How do you know if you are suffering from codependency (coexisting dependencies)? We have described the signs, symptoms, and complications of the disease. The following groups of self-assessment characteristics deal with each group of symptoms and complications.

Characteristics of Denial

❏ 1. Do you avoid reflecting on unpleasant thoughts?

❏ 2. Are you a Pollyanna about difficulties?

❏   3. Do you withdraw into reveries to fulfill needs?

❏   4. Do you exhibit magical thinking or superstitious beliefs?

❏   5. Are you minimally introspective with a barren inner world?

❏   6. Do you fabricate events to bolster self-illusions?

❏   7. If you are not introspective, do you internalize experiences poorly?

❏   8. Do you minimize?

❏   9. Do you see things as they are or the way you wished they were?

❏ 10. Are you irritated by others' assessment of you or the manner in which you behave?

❏ 11. Are you frequently very confused by what's happening in your life?

Characteristics of Emotional Repression

❏   1. Do you have trouble showing your feelings?

❏   2. Are you phlegmatic and lacking in spontaneity?

❏   3. Do you procrastinate and put things off?

❏   4. Do you appear lethargic and lacking in vitality?

❏   5. Are you emotionally impassive or unaffectionate?

❏   6. Are you cold and humorless but edgy?

❏   7. Do you have mood shifts from dejection to anger to apathy?

❏   8. Are you unable to experience pleasure in depth?

❏   9. Do you restrain warmth and affection?

❏   10. Do you vacillate between being anguished and numb?

❏   11. Do you try to keep emotions under tight control?

Characteristics of Compulsion

❏   1. Do you seem attracted to risk, danger, and harm?

❏   2. Do you maintain a regulated and highly organized lifestyle?

❏   3. Are you excessively devoted to work/productivity?

❏   4. Do you suffer from eating disorders?

❏   5. Do you suffer from nicotine addiction?

❏   6. Do you suffer from sexual preoccupation and/or acting out?

❏ 7. Do you suffer from exercise excess?

❏ 8. Do you suffer from gambling and/or spending problems?

❏ 9. Are you an excessive caretaker?

❏ 10. Are you highly self-disciplined?

❏ 11. Do you have chronic feelings of emptiness or boredom?

❏ 12. Do you actively seek attention and solicit praise?

❏ 13. Are you competitive and power-oriented?

❏ 14. Do you sustain monogamous relationships?

❏ 15. Do you insist others do things your way?

❏ 16. Do you constantly seek recognition and admiration?

Characteristics of Low Self-Worth

❏ 1. Do you volunteer to do unpleasant tasks to gain approval?

❏ 2. Do you anxiously anticipate ridicule/humiliation?

❏ 3. Have you made suicidal threats or attempts?

❏ 4. Do you undermine your own good fortunes?

❏   5. Do you place yourself in inferior or demeaning
      positions?

❏   6. Do you act arrogantly self-assured and super
      confident?

❏   7. Do you fail to complete tasks beneficial to
      yourself?

❏   8. Do you feel dejected or guilty after positive
      experiences?

❏   9. Are you compliant, submissive, and placating?

❏ 10. Are you uninterested in people who treat you well?

❏ 11. Do you appear indifferent to praise or criticism?

❏ 12. Do you engage in self-sacrifice and martyrdom?

❏ 13. Do you feel helpless or uncomfortable when alone?

❏ 14. Do you chase after people who treat you poorly?

Characteristics of Relationship Problems

❏   1. Do you seem socially aloof and remote?

❏   2. Do you have difficulty doing things on your own?

❏   3. Do you tend to socially isolate?

❏   4. Do you control interpersonal relationships?

❏   5. Are you relationship dependent?

❏   6. Do you go to great lengths to avoid being alone?

❏   7. Do you provoke rejection, then feel hurt or humiliated?

❏   8. Are you devastated when close relationships end?

❏   9. Are you fearful of loss or desertion?

❏   10. Are you drawn to relationships in which you will suffer?

❏   11. Do you have close friends or intimates?

❏   12. Do you stay in problem relationships because you fear abandonment?

❏   13. Do you have a pattern of unstable and intense relationships?

Characteristics of Organ Dysfunction

❏   1. Do you show little desire for sexual experience?

❏   2. Do you frequently worry about your heart, blood pressure, or having cancer?

❏   3. Are you preoccupied about the shape or appearance of your body?

❑   4. Do you visit a physician frequently for different problems?

❑   5. Do you have high blood pressure or heart irregularities?

❑   6. Do you have numerous stomach, bowel, and bladder problems?

❑   7. Do you have numerous headaches, insomnia, or backaches?

❑   8. Have you had actual organ damage—heart attack, ulcers, or arthritis?

If you find that many of these characteristics apply to you and are uncomfortable or painful in your life but not disabling, then it might serve you well to apply Plan 1 for Recovery (see page 150). However, if you find your characteristics are becoming increasingly painful and more disabling, then you might want to move to Plan 2 for Recovery (on page 150).

Plans for Recovery

Plan 1

1. Join one or two different 12-step support groups to address the more disabling primary compulsions. Fit all other compulsions into these two meetings. Find groups that concentrate on solutions, not problems.

Plan 2

2. Seek treatment with someone specifically trained in codependency treatment. Treat your recovery as you would any other medical recovery: intensive care, aftercare, and a change to a healthy lifestyle. You might choose an outpatient therapist, an outpatient program or an intensive residential program.

How to Choose a Therapist or Treatment Program

It is important to interview a potential therapist or the head of therapy programs. Some suggested questions are:

1. Have you and/or your staff received specific training in treating codependency?

2. Are you and/or your staff free of nicotine, alcohol, and drug abuse?

3. Are you and/or your staff supportive of 12-step self-help groups?

4. Are you and/or your staff trained in experiential therapy (Gestalt, psychodrama, etc.)?

CHAPTER 10

Study Group Guidelines

Group Study Guides for
Understanding Codependency

Codependency recovery is possible and recovery rates run high. One of the best tools for finding a fully ongoing recovery is the daily use of the 12 steps of recovery of Alcoholics Anonymous and Al-Anon as guides for living problems. Additionally, the use of professional and self-help groups is one of the best tools for aiding ourselves in over-coming our distorted thinking.

Twelve-step study groups have found it useful to examine each aspect of their disorder and recovery process. Using group insight and sharing enhances the benefits of individual study. As recovery proceeds, new perspectives and increased insight and emotional sharing results from repeating the study sessions. Emotional pain diminishes as self-worth and gratitude increase.

The following ten suggested study sessions will help a group to stimulate risk taking and sharing. Understanding, self-awareness, hope, and relief of emotional pain begin to take place. The ten suggested study sessions are each coordinated with certain chapters in the book and are broken into:

- Introduction/Self-Assessment

- Explanation

- Discussion

- Into Action

As in book study groups or 12-step study groups, group reading sets the tone and invites participation by members. A leader of the group might begin with the Introduction/Self-Assessment and then invite group member(s) to share reading parts of the Explanation. This is then followed by spontaneous Discussion, after which the group leader can share the Into Action statement as a summary of the study session.

Study Session 1:
THE TRAP

Introduction/Self-Assessment

Do I feel that I live my life going in circles, repeating the same mistakes, stuck in situations I don't want to be in but afraid to change? Do I hurt a lot, perhaps not even knowing why? Does gratitude, feeling good about myself, and excitement with living only come to me in spurts followed by more hurts?

Explanation

Read together Chapter 2 as on page 19, "The Codependency Trap."

Discussion

Suggestion: Group members share examples of substance and/or behavioral medicators that have increased in frequency of use, duration, intensity, and variety.

Into Action

"Now is the time to realize that I'm tired of the way it is and I need to begin a diligent search to understand the trap of my present disorder and what I can do about it! I have work to do!"

Study Session 2: DENIAL

Introduction/Self-Assessment

How does denial work? What is it? Do I do it? Are many of my attitudes, opinions, and behaviors a form of denying reality, the way it really is?

Read together Chapter 6, "Sorting Out Codependency" and "Characteristics of Denial," in Chapter 9.

Explanation

Read together, "Symptoms Group One: Denial/Delusion (Distorted Thinking)" at the beginning of Chapter 4.

Discussion

Suggestion: Participants share recent examples of their denial and minimizing.

Into Action

"Now is the time to accept reality by keeping an open mind and listening to the opinions of others regarding my denial and minimizing. Now is the time for total self-honesty!"

Study Session 3:
EMOTIONAL REPRESSION

Introduction/Self-Assessment

What feelings am I avoiding and keeping inside? Am I honest with myself and others about my anger, hurts, fears, loneliness, and so on? Do I really know what feelings are and what their purpose is? Can I actually recognize a feeling?

Read together "Characteristics of Emotional Repression," in Chapter 9, pages 144–145.

Explanation

Read together "Symptoms Group Two: Emotional Repression (Distorted Feelings)," in Chapter 4, pages 54–62.

Discussion

Suggestion: Participants share rules regarding emotions in their family of origin and how those rules still have power.

Into Action

"Now is the time to let myself feel my feelings in a safe manner and in a safe place. Being in a group may be one of the first places where I can begin to recapture and use my feeling life."

Study Session 4:
COMPULSIVE BEHAVIOR

Introduction/Self-Assessment

What compulsive behaviors do I use to keep my feelings medicated, to give me a temporary high, or to minimize the low? What substances (e.g., alcohol, drugs, nicotine, etc.) do I use or what people, institutions, or occupations do I use to make me feel worthwhile? Do self-defeating, compulsive, repetitive behaviors (e.g., workaholism, control and compulsive caretaking, overeating, not eating, purging, sexual acting out, shopping, gambling, excess exercise, etc.) keep me busy, distracted, and unable to make new choices and changes?

Read together "Characteristics of Compulsion" in Chapter 9, pages 145–146.

Explanation

Read together "Symptoms Group Three: Compulsions (Distorted Behavior)," in Chapter 4, pages 63–70.

Discussion

Suggestion: Participants share their "Big Three" compulsions that they have been dependent on at one time or another. Identify them as coexisting dependencies (codependency), whether they are dependencies on substances, behaviors, or a combination of both.

Into Action

"Now is the time to stop medicating myself with repetitive self-defeating behaviors. I cannot heal what I cannot feel, and I cannot feel what I medicate. If I can stop these behaviors, I will. If I cannot stop these behaviors, or I trade them for more destructive and disabling ones, I will seek professional care for help."

Study Session 5:
LOW SELF-WORTH

Introduction/Self-Assessment

Do I struggle with my self-worth? Is it difficult to make choices and act on my own behalf? Many of us have been reprimanded for being self-centered and conceited without explaining the difference between this and a high level of self-worth and self-confidence. We are taught and learn on our own to deprecate ourselves, many times to the degree that when some bad event befalls us, we say, "I probably deserved that."

Read together "Characteristics of Low Self-Worth," in Chapter 9, pages 146–147.

Explanation

Read together "Complications Group One: Low Self-Worth (Disabled Spirituality)" in Chapter 5, pages 75–83.

Discussion

Suggestion: Participants share their perceptions of themselves at different ages, or participants discuss current experiences between humility and humiliation and self-worth and vanity.

Into Action

"Now is the time for me to accept myself, especially my inner childlike self, as a worthy person. As I share more about myself and find myself acceptable to those around me, I can accept myself more fully and believe in my own worth."

Study Session 6: RELATIONSHIPS

Introduction/Self-Assessment

Have I become too dependent on others, especially certain others (lover, friends, boss, heroes, professionals, etc.), so that I now feel and appear unsafe and needy? Or have I begun to isolate and resist intimacy? In either case, I am spending a great amount of time preoccupied with and controlling others. Either way, dependent or isolated, it is probably the result of not having a good relationship with myself. A healthy relationship requires a healthy self.

Read together "Characteristics of Relationship Problems" in Chapter 9, pages 147–148.

Explanation

Read together "Complications Group Two: Relationship Problems (Disabled Living)" in Chapter 5, pages 83–88.

Discussion

Suggestion: Participants share their use of control, enmeshment, dependency, isolation, and aloofness in their relationships. The key words are:

Intimacy	Fight and flight
Passion	Independence

Into Action

"Now is the time for me to grow in knowledge about myself. It is important for me to think for myself, to feel and share my feelings, even when risky. As I learn to maintain myself, I can better maintain my emotional investments in friendships and relationships. As I learn to better maintain relationships, I am then best prepared for a meaningful and healthful primary relationship."

Study Session 7:
MEDICAL PROBLEMS

Introduction/Self-Assessment

Has my codependency affected my health? Has or does my body suffer from stress-related disorders? Am I so caught up in surviving, watching, scrambling, and worrying that I fail to maintain good health habits and follow healthy eating, sleeping, and exercise patterns? Am I ignoring signals my body may be sending me, signals that might be saying "slow down," "check this out," or "something needs fixing"?

Read together "Characteristics of Organ Dysfunction," in Chapter 9, pages 148–149.

Explanation

Read together, "Complications Group Three: Medical Problems (Disabled Physical Functioning)" in Chapter 5, pages 88–92.

Discussion

Suggestion: Participants share any preoccupations with body image, sleep patterns, energy patterns, their last visit to their physician/dentist, and past histories of stress-related disorders. They also share physical recovery stories.

Into Action

"Now is the time to take good care of myself in every way, including physically. I will pay attention to what I eat, and I will commit to regular exercise and regular medical and dental care as a part of my recovery program."

Study Session 8:
CHOICES AND RISKS

Introduction/Self-Assessment

Have my compulsions robbed me of the power of choice? Am I so busy "doing" that I am unable to hold still and just be? Is my fear of loss and abandonment so great that I am powerless to make the very choices and changes that would eliminate my compulsions and fears? Recovery demands choices and changes. Choices and changes demand risk taking without a guarantee. Can I make a choice without a guarantee that it's the right choice? Do I have the faith that I am able to make a choice that is the right choice? And if it seems not to be the right choice, am I able to learn from that and move on to further choice making?

Reread together "Characteristics of Compulsion" in Chapter 9, pages 145–146.

Explanation

Read together the following excerpt from *Choicemaking* by Sharon Wegscheider-Cruse.

Does the Ideal Choicemaker go his/her own way alone, aloof, carefree, and independent? Not at all. Choicemakers stay concerned and interested in others, but Choicemakers do not allow that concern and care to become the center of their existence. As Choicemakers we will direct our own lives as much as possible, without seeking control over others and without letting ourselves be subservient to another's opinions or feelings.

We will learn to decide if we want to have a career or stay at home. A choice, not an expectation.

We will decide whether to adhere to family traditions or start some of our own.

We will choose whether to have a career change or stay with an early-chosen profession.

We will learn to take care of ourselves and negotiate our involvement in relationships.

As Choicemakers we won't necessarily always like what we see each other do or what we hear each other say. But we'll feel free to share with fellow Choicemakers what we don't like for the sole purpose of sharing or enhancing understanding. We are not to remold others in our image. In respect for each other's personhood, we will let each other decide whether to change or not. Anything less in this sharing process is covered-up manipulation.

Once we succeed in taking the first steps toward our own freedom in personal responsibility, we can choose to share our "self" with someone else in a relationship of our choice. We won't just fall in love with someone, we won't be mindlessly swept away. We will find someone we can choose to love.

As Choicemakers, we will cultivate friendships that are rewarding, mutually enriching. We will learn the value of choosing to move away from relationships that bring us down, that thwart our self-worth. We will learn to abandon, if necessary, lifestyles encumbered with negative thoughts and feelings. As Choicemakers, we take the initiative to surround ourselves with individuals who bring out the very best in us and help us on our inner journey toward goodness, love, and inner peace ...

Our imperfections have a symptom—pain. And pain signals dysfunction, injury, or some disease that requires something to change before relief can occur. That something is frequently us. One of the more unexpected side effects of change turns out to be growth.

But there are times when that pain is like a rock in our shoe—almost imperceptible, bearable, and unimportant, as compared to the immediate task at hand. Then after we remove it, its actual importance becomes clear. Now we see the deep impression it has made, and almost immediately we feel the relief and freedom and regained agility when we remove the rock. We look at our wounds and blisters in disbelief that we could have denied their seriousness, or even their presence, and certainly their influence for so long.

But no matter the number of stones that find their way into our shoes, the human spirit, once enlightened, continues to look up and hope and learn and delight in each lesson. The human spirit continues to choose and change—and continues to remove stones one by one.

CHOICEMAKING

EVERY DAY I HAVE BEFORE ME MANY CHOICES,
IT IS NOT EASY TO CHOOSE,
FOR OFTEN THE CHOICE MEANS LETTING GO
OF THE PAST
OF THE PRESENT

I KNOW WHAT THE PAST WAS.
I KNOW WHAT THE PRESENT IS.
BUT CHOICE PROPELS ME INTO THE FUTURE.
I'M NOT SURE I'LL MAKE THE RIGHT CHOICES.

IT'S NOT EASY TO "LET GO."
IT'S NOT EASY TO FLY INTO THE FUTURE.
IT'S LIKE THE SPACE BETWEEN TRAPEZES.

It's not knowing whether you're going to be caught.
It's not knowing whether you're going to fall.

It's not easy to live in trust.
That space between trapezes requires faith.
I must admit that my faith is often shaky.
I pray and hope that I'll make good decisions,
That I'll be caught and will not fall.

Every day I have before me many choices.

To become healthy, to become whole means that one must take responsibility for oneself. One must become a Choicemaker every step of the way. For a codependent who has spent years watching, weighing alternatives, afraid to make a mistake . . . often passively waiting for others to decide . . . becoming a Choicemaker can be a formidable task.

Yet Choicemaking is the foundation that recovery builds on. Choicemaking makes recovery possible.

Discussion

Suggestion: Participants share their most difficult recent choice and a possible future choice. They also discuss how choicemaking changes as recovery continues.

Into Action

"Now is the time to want to change. If I haven't liked the way my life is going, then I must make changes in it and me. Changes are dependent on choices, and choices are needed now."

Study Session 9:
FORGIVENESS AND AMENDS

Introduction/Self-Assessment

Full recovery means letting go of old bitterness and resentments. The emotions of bitterness drain our energy and cloud our thinking. Those for whom we hold resentment live in our heads rent free. Have I forgiven those who have wronged me? Am I preoccupied with past injuries done to me, even those of long ago? And do I still carry pain, shame, and guilt for the wrongs I have done to others?

Explanation

Many times we have apologized and many times others have apologized to us. The need for the ongoing use of our ability to forgive and to be forgiven is extremely important in our recovery. Many times we fail to remember that we have the capacity and ability—and even the need—to forgive others and to accept their request for us to forgive them. Forgiveness is almost always a two-way street. If you cannot make amends, you suffer. If you cannot accept amends from others, you also suffer. If you cannot accept an apology, then you cannot forgive. An apology is a request for your forgiveness.

If you cannot request another person's forgiveness, then it is likely that you are not ready to forgive them if they refuse your request. It sounds complicated and as if it is going in a circle, but it really isn't circular; rather, it is like a tennis match. It only takes one to serve, and that's all a person can do. If a serve is returned, then there is a match. Both individuals benefit. But if no one receives your serve, there is no match.

If you have made an apology to someone and have asked for their forgiveness and they have failed to forgive you, then no further action is necessary on your part. No two-way negotiation will take place. Even so, you can receive relief from your fear, anger, and resentment toward them and the events that caused you discomfort in the first place. Such relief often comes by simply asking for their forgiveness. Whether or not you receive it, it pays to practice your serve. One exercise that we have found helpful is to make a list of:

1. Some people who have hurt you in your life need to ask for your forgiveness. If they do, can you forgive them?

2. Some people whom you have hurt need you to ask for their forgiveness. Can you do it?

3. Some words that describe how you feel or what you do when you have been hurt.

4. Some people whom you have seen suffer from their inability to forgive. List the number of years it's been since the event occurred in which they have been unable to forgive.

The exercise part of this is if you are unable to do number 1 or perform number 2, you will probably also feel number 3 for the number of years you listed in number 4.

Discussion

Suggestion: Participants can share any new awareness and feelings that arose from doing the exercises. A forgiveness plan can be made.

Into Action

"Now is the time for me to realistically look at how much of my emotional energy is unnecessarily spent mulling over old resentments and the guilt I carry for not having made proper amends. Now is the time to understand that I can heal through making the proper amends and being prepared to receive amends from others. I must now identify my needs and desires, which will require that I identify all the losses, both real and unreal. For those real losses, I must grieve the loss and feel the pain. To avoid the pain is to avoid an emotion, to avoid reality, and therefore to start chasing a myth. I realize that forgiveness can only come about in reality. This is the time to make a list of all those I have harmed and to be willing to make amends to them whenever possible, except when to do so would injure them or others (as suggested in Step 9 of the 12 Steps of Alcoholics Anonymous)."

Study Session 10:
RECOVERY AND LIVING

Introduction/Self-Assessment

The happiness we all seek from recovery can sometimes escape us if we overdo the process. Our search for the very best path or exactly the right answers results in a constant searching pattern, which causes us to pass up good methods of recovery that would work perfectly well if we would just stop and let them. Until we stop chasing after solutions or stop working on problems rather than through problems, we cannot help anyone else in their recovery. We cannot give away or share that which we do not have. Am I still on a frantic search? Do I still shrug off opportunities to recover because they don't seem just right for me? Am I a good example to others of how to live life? Am I ready to enjoy the benefits of truly giving to others, of doing someone a favor without being found out?

Explanation

Read together Chapter 7, "Treatment and Recovery." Also read portions of "Love" by Bill W. in Chapter 8 on pages 137–141.

Discussion

Suggestion: Participants can now develop a Care Plan for themselves in front of the group and with input from the group.

Into Action

"Now is the time for me to set limits on the acute process of recovery. I will always have a program of living, but I do not want a lifetime or lifestyle of therapy. My life will become centered and balanced so I will be able to become a full-fledged participant in life with those I choose, in the places I choose, and at the times I choose. Then I will have much to offer and will experience the joy of helping each time I pass it on."

It is hoped that the suggestions in these lesson plans are useful to you and other members of a group you may attend or that you organize.

The concepts in this book are exciting and useful. New information about the brain, psychology and healthy thinking, feeling and behaving continues to evolve. The brain is the primary organ of all of our functioning. It is a powerful and awesome organ. It is ours to use and, hopefully, through the insights and lessons in this book, we will always use it and treat it well.

BIBLIOGRAPHY

Ackerman, Robert J. *Perfect Daughters: Adult Daughters of Alcoholics*. Deerfield Beach, FL: Health Communications, 1989.

Ackerman, Robert J., and Susan E. Pickering. *Abused No More: Recovery for Women from Abusive or Co-dependent Relationships*. Blue Ridge Summit, PA: Tab Books, 1989.

Ashton, Heather. *Brain Systems Disorders and Psychotropic Drugs*. Oxford, UK: Oxford University Press, 1987.

Cermak, Timmen L. *A Time to Heal: The Road to Recovery for Adult Children of Alcoholics*. New York: Avon Books, 1988.

Cloninger, C. Robert. "A Systematic Method for Clinical Description and Classification of Personality Variants." *Archives of General Psychiatry* (June 1987).

Coyle, Joseph T. "Neuroscience and Psychiatry." In *Textbook of Psychiatry*. Washington, DC: American Psychiatric Press, 1988.

Cruse, Joseph R. *Painful Affairs: Looking for Love through Addiction and Codependency*. Deerfield Beach, FL: Health Communications, 1989.

Cruse, Joseph R., Sharon Wegscheider, and George Bougher. *Experiential Therapy for Co-dependency*. Onsite Training.

Diagnostic and Statistical Manual III-R. Washington, DC: American Psychiatric Association, 1987.

Elliott, Robert, Jeanne Watson, Rhonda Goldman, and Leslie Greenberg. *Learning Emotion-Focused Therapy: The Process-Experiential Approach to Change*. Washington, DC: American Psychiatric Association, 2009.

Engel, Jorgen. *Brain Reward Systems and Abuse*. New York: Raven Press, 1987.

Gorski, Terence T. "Defining Co-dependence." Paper presented at National Forum on Co-dependence, Scottsdale, Arizona, September 1989.

Kabat-Zinn, Jon. *Coming to Our Senses: Healing Ourselves and the World through Mindfulness*. New York: Hyperion, 2006.

———. *Full Catastrophe Living: Using the Wisdom of Your Body and Mind to Face Stress, Pain, and Illness*. 1st ed. New York: Delacorte Press, 1990.

———. *Wherever You Go There You Are*. New York: Hyperion, 2005.

Kuhn, Thomas. *The Structure of Scientific Revolutions*. 3rd ed. Chicago: University of Chicago Press, 1996.

Mahrer, Alvin, Ph.D., *The Complete Guide to Experiential Psychotherapy*. Boulder, CO: Bull Publishing Company, 2003.

Millon, Theodore. *Millon Clinical Multiaxial Inventory-II: Manual for the MCMI-II*. 2nd ed. Minneapolis, MN: National Computer Systems, 1987.

———. "Personalogic Psychotherapy: Ten Commandments for a Post-eclectic Approach to Integrative Treatment." Paper presented at the Annual Meeting of the Society for the Exploration of Psychotherapy Integration, Evanston, Illinois, May 1987.

Millon, Theodore, and George S. Everly Jr. *Personality and Its Disorders: A Biosocial Learning Approach*. New York: Wiley, 1985.

Restak, Richard M. *The Mind*. New York: Bantam, 1988.

Selye, Hans. *Stress in Health and Disease*. Oxford, UK: Butterworth-Heinemann Ltd., 1976.

———. *The Stress of Life*. 2nd ed. New York: McGraw-Hill, 1978.

———. *Stress without Distress*. New York: Signet, 1975.

Stone, Evelyn M. *American Psychiatric Glossary*. Washington, DC: American Psychiatric Press, 1988.

Washton, Arnold, and Donna Boundy. *Willpower's Not Enough: Understanding and Recovering from Addiction of Every Kind*. New York: Harper & Row, 1989.

Wegscheider, Sharon. *Another Chance: Hope and Healing for the Alcoholic Family*. Palo Alto, CA: Science and Behavior Books, 1981.

———. *Coupleship*. Deerfield Beach, FL: Health Communications, 1988.

———. *The Family Trap*. Rapid City, SD: Nurturing Networks, 1976.

———. *Learning to Love Yourself* 2nd ed. Deerfield Beach, FL: Health Communications, 2012.

ABOUT THE AUTHORS

Joseph Cruse, M.D., is an addiction medicine specialist, author, writer, and lecturer. He is the founding medical director of the Betty Ford Center. He served as president of the medical staff at Eisenhower Hospital and as a medical director of Onsite Workshops. He has consulted for corporations, school systems, hospitals, and alcohol and drug treatment centers. He has appeared on *60 Minutes*, *Good Morning America*, and *The Late Night Show*.

Sharon Wegscheider-Cruse is a nationally known consultant, educator, and author of seventeen books, many of which have been translated into French, German, Spanish, Greek, Portuguese, and Japanese. She was the founding chairperson of the National Association for Children of Alcoholics and the founder of Onsite Workshops in Tennessee. As a family therapist she has conducted workshops around the world consulting with the military, school systems, business and industry, treatment centers, and corporations. She is a past winner of the Marty Mann award as a top communicator and has appeared on *The Phil Donahue Show*, *The Oprah Winfrey Show* twice and *Good Morning America*. She is the subject of several DVDs used for training purposes. Sharon lives in Las Vegas. Sharon and her books are available at www.sharonwcruse.com.

INDEX